Social Studies Alive!®

Solutions for Effective Instruction

A Sourcebook for Integrating
Language Arts Skills and Strategies

Chief Executive Officer: Bert Bower

Chief Operating Officer: Amy Larson

Director of Product Development: Liz Russell

Managing Editor: Laura Alavosus

Project Editor: Carol Domblewski

Editorial Associates: Anna Embree, Sarah Sudano

Production Manager: Lynn Sanchez

Design Manager: Jeff Kelly

Graphic Designer: Victoria Philp

Contributing Writers: Carol Domblewski, Chris Garcia

Photography
Title page:
T: Marina Jefferson/Getty Images
M: David Olsen/Getty Images
B: RF/Getty Images

TCi™

Teachers' Curriculum Institute
P.O. Box 50996
Palo Alto, CA 94303

Customer Service: 800-497-6138
www.teachtci.com

ISBN 978-1-58371-749-3
1 2 3 4 5 6 7 8 9 10 -MLI- 15 14 13 12 11 10

Part One

Teaching Language Arts Skills

Identify Cause-and-Effect Relationships

Exploring cause and effect deepens students' understanding of events, concepts, and themes in history, economics, geography, and civics. Using the skill helps students understand that there are often multiple causes for, or effects of, a historical or other event. As they apply this skill, students also learn to think about causation over time, including both immediate and long-term causes and effects.

Teach the Skill Post a list of words and phrases that show cause-and-effect relationships, including the following: *cause, effect, affect, as a result, because, brought about, consequently, due to, for, led to, since, so, so that,* and *therefore.* Select a good example of a cause-effect passage from the text that embeds some of these signal words. Help students look for these words as they read and determine the causes and effects that the signal words help point out.

If the passage you select presents a single cause with one or more effects, project *Solutions Master 1: Cause-and-Effect Diagram.* Have volunteers identify how to label the boxes and how to fill them in. If the passage presents a chain of causes and effects, project *Solutions Master 2: Cause-and-Effect Chain.* Have volunteers identify how to label the boxes and how to fill them in. After you complete the organizer and review what it shows, project the alternative cause-and-effect organizer and explain how students might use it for a slightly different type of text.

Practice the Skill Point out another paragraph or section of the text that is organized or developed by cause and effect (such as Grade 3, page 46, paragraph 2). Distribute copies of the appropriate cause-and-effect Solutions Master and have students work individually or in pairs to complete it. Discuss the results as a class.

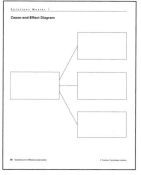

Solutions Master 1:
Cause-and-Effect Diagram

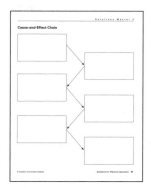

Solutions Master 2:
Cause-and-Effect Chain

Classify/Categorize

When students classify, they explore relationships by generating either the class or the members (or examples) of a class; for example, students may classify types of governments, legal systems, or economic systems by generating examples. Conversely, they may classify by grouping a list of concepts such as *economist, historian,* and *social scientist* (Grade 4) under a single heading, such as "careers related to social studies." Classification provides practice with new concepts and vocabulary, and may increase students' ability to link new ideas with known ones.

Teach the Skill Present a list of items to be classified into one or more categories, such as a list of landforms. After students come up with this first and simple level of classification by titling their list, note that landforms can also be classified according to whether they are land or water landforms. Project *Solutions Master 3:*

Two-Column Chart. Have volunteers identify how to label the columns and how to fill in the chart. Point out that students may also, at times, use a chart with three or more columns to classify or categorize.

Explain that students will sometimes come across transitional phrases in their reading that signal categories or classes. These include phrases such as *the first type, another group, one kind, other kinds, other sorts,* and *one type.* Write these phrases on the board, or present them as the beginning of sentence frames, and invite students to use two or more of them orally to talk with a partner about the landforms they just classified.

During writing practice or instruction, you can transfer classification and categorization skills to the task of writing paragraphs by noting how the category often becomes part of the topic sentence, while the things that belong in the category often create the content of the supporting sentences.

Practice the Skill List the thirteen colonies (Grade 5) or members of categories or classes that you are studying now. Have students determine two, three, or more categories into which to sort them. Obvious categories for the thirteen colonies example include the New England Colonies, the Middle Colonies, and the Southern Colonies, but students may also work creatively to categorize or classify. Discuss the categories they create, and decide which are most useful for understanding history, geography, government, economics, or the lives of citizens. Talk about how the groupings or categories can help students with other skills, such as making generalizations and comparing and contrasting.

Solutions Master 3:
Two-Column Chart

Compare and Contrast

When students compare and contrast, they may both review and generate likenesses and differences between two or more people, places, events, or things. In doing so, they often deepen their understanding of conflicts, movement, regions, change, and other major themes in civic life as well as history, geography, and government.

Teach the Skill Talk about how students know when they are reading a paragraph or section of their text that compares and/or contrasts. Elicit a list of words, such as the following, that show comparison, and write them on the board: *also, and, another, as well, like, likewise, same, similarly,* and *too.* Do the same with transitional and other words and phrases that show contrast, such as *although, but, differ, different, however, in spite of, instead, nevertheless, nonetheless, on the other hand,* and *yet.* Select a good example of a comparison, contrast, or comparison-contrast passage from the text that embeds some of these signal words, and have students look for these words as they read. Then ask them to name the comparisons or contrasts that the signal words help point out.

If the passage you present shows both comparisons and contrasts, project *Solutions Master 4: Venn Diagram.* Have volunteers identify how to label the circles and how to fill them in. If there are just comparisons or just contrasts in the passage, project *Solutions Master 3: Two-Column Chart* or *Solutions Master 5: Three-Column Chart* as appropriate. Have volunteers identify how to label the

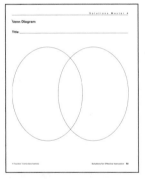

Solutions Master 4:
Venn Diagram

Solutions Master 5:
Three-Column Chart

columns and how to fill them in. After you complete the organizer and review what it shows, project the alternative comparison and contrast organizers and explain how students might use them for slightly different types of text.

Practice the Skill Select two concepts currently under study for students to compare and contrast. For example, students might compare two regions. Divide the class into five small groups and distribute a copy of *Solutions Master 4: Venn Diagram* to each group. Assign each group one of the following categories: landforms, economic activities, resources, or culture. Challenge groups to record similarities and differences between the two regions within their category.

Call on a person from each group to report the group's findings to the whole class. Ask: *In which categories are the regions most similar? In which categories are they most different?* Lead a discussion about how the comparisons and contrasts help students understand the regions.

Sequence

When students sequence, they put events or steps in a process in time order. Sequencing may be a first step in developing historical perspective or in formulating historical questions. It may also help students make links between long-term and/or immediate causes and effects.

Teach the Skill Post a list of words and phrases that show time order, including the following: *after, before, during, earlier, eventually, finally, first, later, meanwhile, next, then,* and *when.* Select a good example of a sequence passage from the text that embeds some of these signal words. Have students look for these words as they read the passage; also ask them to determine the order of events that the signal words help point out. Then project *Solutions Master 6: Sequence Chain,* and have students explain how to arrange these events in order on the transparency. Record their answers, and then work with students to give the sequence chain a title.

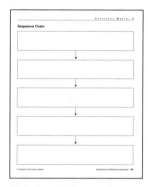

Solutions Master 6:
Sequence Chain

Sequencing should also be taught with the use of dates and other words that show the specific passage of time. For example, you might have students skim a chapter about the growing tensions between the colonies and Great Britain to identify key dates, such as 1765, 1770, 1773, and 1774 (Grade 5). Then project *Solutions Master 7: Timeline/Judgment Graphic* and model how you would use it to sequence dates, as well as the events that occurred on those dates. Be sure to work with students to give the timeline a title.

Practice the Skill Point out another paragraph or section of the text that is organized sequentially or chronologically. Distribute copies of *Solutions Master 6: Sequence Chain* or *Solutions Master 7: Timeline/Judgment Graphic,* and have students work individually or in pairs to complete it and title it. Discuss the results as a class.

Solutions Master 7:
Timeline/Judgment Graphic

Make Inferences

Making inferences means reading between the lines. When students make inferences, they arrive at a meaning that is implied in the text but not directly stated there. The skill is closely related to the skill of drawing conclusions in that students must draw on or synthesize textual information in order to infer. Inferences differ from conclusions, however, in that inferences always require students to use their own prior knowledge or experience. Furthermore, an inference is often based on a small amount of information, such as a sentence or two. It is often most useful in assessing motivation or other personal characteristics. Conclusions, on the other hand, often result from reading longer amounts of text, such as whole sections or chapters. Conclusions sometimes also result from combining textual information without taking personal experience or judgments into account.

Teach the Skill Project *Solutions Master 8: Inference/Conclusion Diagram* and label the first box *Fact(s) from the Text*. Select and write a factual sentence or two about a topic under study from which students can draw an inference. For example, in the Facts box, write, *Columbus told his frightened men to be patient. He was sure Asia wasn't far away* (Grade 5). Then ask students what they already know about someone who can act, feel, or think differently from others, especially when others are frightened. Students might infer that such a person is confident or sure of himself or herself, a good leader, or, possibly, very far from understanding reality. Record the information they add in the second box, and label it *What I Already Know*. Then ask students what inference they can make about Columbus, such as, *Columbus was sure of himself;* record it in the final box; and label the final box *Inference*. Reinforce the idea that the inference is based on text information and is logical, but it is not stated directly in the text.

Practice the Skill Present another example of information from the text from which it is possible to draw an inference, such as specific information about American Indian cultures (Grade 5). Have students form pairs, and distribute a copy of *Solutions Master 8: Inference/Conclusion Diagram* to each pair. Have pairs complete the organizer and share and compare their inference with the inferences of other pairs. Review the process of making inferences, as well as the results, as a class.

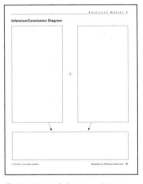

Solutions Master 8:
Inference/Conclusion Diagram

Draw Conclusions

When students draw conclusions, they put ideas and concepts together in order to make a new statement that goes beyond what they learned. Drawing conclusions requires students to read or listen carefully and to focus on facts. It often requires them to ask questions about what they are learning, as well as to draw on prior knowledge. It always requires original and critical thinking as students decide how the facts work together to lead to a single statement about their meaning.

Teach the Skill Tell students that a conclusion is an idea that they come to after learning new facts from reading or listening. Explain that, often, but not always, their conclusion comes from both those new facts they learn and what they already know. Project *Solutions Master 8: Inference/Conclusion Diagram*. Ask students, for example, for the facts about how land is used in the Southeast (Grade 4). List their ideas in the first box, and label it *Facts*. Then point to the second box. Tell students that they should add additional facts here, which might come from prior knowledge, or what they already know, or from the textbook. Distribute a copy of *Solutions Master 8: Inference/Conclusion Diagram* to each student. Have them copy the facts from the transparency, and work on their own or in pairs to complete the second box. Review the ideas they came up with. Choose one or more to record in the second box of the projected transparency. Label it *More Facts*. Then model drawing a conclusion by putting together the facts in both boxes. Write the conclusion in the final box and label it *Conclusion*. Have a volunteer sum up the steps in the process of drawing a conclusion.

Explain that students will sometimes come across transitional phrases in their reading that signal a conclusion. These include words and phrases such as *in conclusion, therefore,* and *thus.* Write these words and phrases on the board, or present them as the beginning of sentence frames, and invite students to use one of them as they sum up the contents of the organizer they just completed.

Practice the Skill Tell students to draw a conclusion about something they already studied or that you have discussed recently as a class. For example, you might ask them what it would be like to live in a different region, such as the Northeast or the Southwest. Have students form pairs, and distribute copies of *Solutions Master 8: Inference/Conclusion Diagram* to each pair. Have them list facts they already know about the region in the first box. Have them list additional facts or prior knowledge in the second box. Then ask them to draw a conclusion about what life would be like for them in that region. As a class, discuss the conclusions and the process of reaching them.

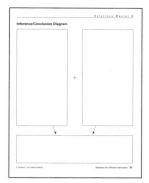

Solutions Master 8:
Inference/Conclusion Diagram

Generalize

Like the skills of making inferences and drawing conclusions, generalizing requires students to understand ideas and facts they read and to combine or synthesize them in order to make an original statement. The resulting statement is a blanket or overview statement about a topic. It carefully and accurately sums up information.

Teach the Skill Explain that students must do a good bit of reading and learning about a topic before they can make a generalization. Even then, it is not always possible to make an accurate generalization because other books or sources may reveal new and different facts about a topic. That is why many of the best generalizations begin with words and phrases such as *many, most of the time, usually,* and *for the most part.* If possible, choose a topic from the textbook, and read it as it is covered there. Then read a second source before beginning the task of making a generalization. Alternatively, select one section or chapter of the text, such as the chapter on global trade (Grade 3). You might then ask students to make a generalization about global trade. Model how you would make a generalization by displaying *Solutions Master 9: Generalization Diagram.* Use the top boxes to record students' ideas about the benefits and problems of global trade. Then note how you use these facts and ideas to make a generalization about the value, impact, or desirability of global trade. Record the generalization in the bottom box.

Explain that students will sometimes come across transitional phrases in their reading that signal a generalization. These include words and phrases such as *in general, overall,* and *in summary.* They also include the qualifying words and phrases *many, most of the time, usually,* and *for the most part.* Write these words and phrases on the board, or present them as the beginning of sentence frames, and invite students to use one of them as they orally sum up the contents of the organizer they just completed.

Practice the Skill Have students practice the skill on their own or with a partner. Distribute copies of *Solutions Master 9: Generalization Diagram* and name a topic you have studied recently or are studying now, such as why Native American groups established different ways of life (Grade 5). Invite students to use the organizer to record facts and then make a generalization about it. Review both the generalizations and the processes students used to arrive at them.

Solutions Master 9:
Generalization Diagram

Analyze

When students analyze, they break an idea or event into its parts. To analyze an argument, students identify the reasons for the writer's or speaker's opinion, as well as the support used to back those reasons up. When students analyze expository writing or speech, they often separate main ideas from details, explanations, and other kinds of development. Analysis is often a first or early step in the process of evaluating. First, students understand, in detail, what something says. Then they make a judgment, or statement of value or worth, about it.

Teach the Skill Tell your students that to *analyze* means "to determine what something is made up of." Display this paragraph on the board or on a transparency, or have students focus on a paragraph of information about natural resources from the textbook (Grades 3, 4, and 5).

> *Natural resources are things found in nature that people use. Water, air, trees, and soil are found in nature. Humans do not make them. People use natural resources to meet their needs. These resources must be protected.*

Project *Solutions Master 10: Web,* and write *Natural Resources* in the center of the web, noting that it is the topic of the passage. Tell students to analyze, or break down the idea of natural resources, by telling you what the paragraph has to say about the topic. As students respond, record their answers in the outer circles, generating more circles as needed. For example, you might use one of the outer circles to write *found in nature* and then create new circles that radiate from that circle to list *water, air, trees,* and *soil.* Use the other outer circles to record other ideas about natural resources. Review what the completed web shows, noting that you have gone through a process of analysis to create it.

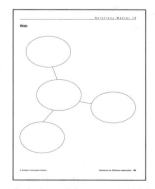

Solutions Master 10: Web

Practice the Skill Choose a concept or topic from a chapter that the class is studying now, such as maps. Have students form small groups to analyze the concept by breaking it down into subtopics, single ideas, categories, as well as the details that make up the subcategories. Distribute copies of *Solutions Master 10: Web* to each group. Have groups share their completed organizers with the class, and discuss how each analyzes, or breaks down into parts, the concept of maps.

Make Decisions

Students make a decision by choosing between two or more things or two or more courses of action. Using the skill helps students evaluate choices made by people in the past as well as in today's world. Students can apply this skill to the choices they make as students, family members, members of other groups or teams, friends, citizens, and consumers.

Teach the Skill Tell students that making decisions is a multi-step process. First, they should identify their goal. For example, a goal might be to elect the best person to office. Then students should name the different choices to reach that goal. Next, they evaluate each choice by thinking about the possible results of each choice or by listing the pros and cons. Finally, after careful consideration and, perhaps, discussion, they make a choice. Project *Solutions Master 11: Decision Tree/Evaluation Chart*. At the top, write the goal. An example might be the goal of electing the best person as a class leader. Then, on the first branches, list two made-up candidates, such as Pete Popular and Keeshona Qualified, and have students suggest what some of their qualities might be. Then ask students for their ideas for pros and cons based on these qualities, such as the ability to talk easily with Pete Popular, Pete Popular's good communication skills, or Keeshona Qualified's record of helping out and being a leader in school projects. Record the pros and cons. Finally, discuss what the pros and cons suggest, have students make an evaluation of the better choice, and record it.

Solutions Master 11:
Decision Tree/Evaluation Chart

Explain that a decision tree can sometimes have many branches. For example, students might want to decide which region of the country they would most like to live in. Note that students can always add branches to a decision tree or create their own decision trees with many branches.

Practice the Skill Distribute copies of *Solutions Master 11: Decision Tree/Evaluation Chart* to pairs of students. Introduce a decision that students have just read about or are about to study such as whether to use fertilizers and pesticides in a backyard or community garden (Grade 4). Remind students of the decision-making steps you used in teaching the skill: *1) Identify the goal. 2) Name choices to reach that goal. 3) Evaluate those choices by listing the pros and cons. 4) Study the pros and cons and make a decision.* Lead a class discussion about students' decisions. Connect their decisions to their goals. Ask students to respectfully evaluate one another's decisions.

Evaluate

When students evaluate, they make judgments. If they are reading history, students might evaluate the decisions people made in the past. If they are reading about the economy or government, they might evaluate current choices. In this respect, evaluating is like decision-making and involves weighing alternatives or pros and cons. Another way in which students can evaluate is by judging a passage's importance, value, or interest to them. Through this process, they interact more deeply with, and make personal connections to, the text.

Teach the Skill Present a choice someone or a group recently made in your school or community, such as to put a new basketball court on the playground. Ask students to discuss why they think this was a good choice. Then present an alternative to that choice, such as spending the money to make the cafeteria more modern or comfortable. Ask: *Which was the better way to spend the town's or city's money? Was the right choice made?* Project *Solutions Master 11: Decision Tree/Evaluation Chart*, and lead students through an evaluation of the choice. As you do so, note that evaluations are not always black and white, and that sometimes they are easier to make long after the events take place than they are at the time when a decision is made. Also, a course of action that is right for one person or group may not be the course of action that is right or best for another person or group.

Solutions Master 11:
Decision Tree/Evaluation Chart

A second way to teach evaluation is to pause after a section or chapter and ask students to make judgments about the value or worth of certain information to them in their own lives. For example, after students read about city hall (Grade 3), they might evaluate by answering questions such as *How useful is this information to you? Why?*

Practice the Skill Present students with a decision made in history, such as the decision to become a Patriot and fight for independence (Grade 5). Project *Solutions Master 11: Decision Tree/Evaluation Chart*, and use it to record the decision, as well as an alternative to that decision. Have students explore the pros and cons of the decision and record their ideas. Discuss their completed charts, and reinforce the idea that it is sometimes easier to make evaluations of choices after the events have taken place.

Predict

When students make predictions in social studies, they usually examine choices that groups, individuals, or leaders face now or have faced in the past. Then students speculate on the effects of different paths people might have taken in the past or different choices they might make now. Students can also predict likely outcomes in relationship to economic concepts, such as supply and demand, as well as in relationship to geographical themes, such as movement and human-environment interaction. The best predictions rely both on understanding of the subject matter, as well as decision-making and evaluation skills.

Teach the Skill Have students examine choices that people make about one of our natural resources such as water. Students might focus on a particular topic in the textbook, such as the water from the Colorado River (Grade 4, Chapter 11). Project *Solutions Master 3: Two-Column Chart* and use it to record students' ideas about some of the choices that people are currently making in terms of water use in the area. Have students use the second column to list alternatives to these choices. Use the completed chart to discuss how or why, or predict when, people might, if ever, turn to the alternatives. Emphasize that predictions must always be based on facts or evidence from a reliable source, although students should bring their experience and prior knowledge to the task of predicting. For each prediction students make, require them to explain how they combined facts and evidence with prior knowledge or experience.

Practice the Skill Have your students predict based on chapter content. For example, have students predict how regions of the country might have been different had different groups of people settled there originally. In this case, students might think about the probable differences in culture, place names, and other ways of life had the Spanish settled in Louisiana or had the English settled in the Southwest.

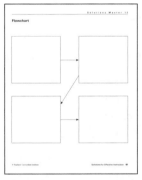

Solutions Master 3:
Two-Column Chart

Solve Problems

The best reason to teach the skill of solving problems is to make it clear to students that good solutions usually don't simply arise; instead, the best solutions are often the result of a careful process. As with the process of writing and other processes, solving problems may require returning to or redoing some steps. Nevertheless, students can learn to break the task down into manageable and clear steps. They can also use what they have learned about evaluating to help them solve problems.

Teach the Skill Ask students to name a problem that needs to be solved in your school or in your community. For example, they might say that your town or city needs more playing fields for soccer, baseball, and other sports. Tell students they have just completed the first step in solving problems, which is naming the problem. Ask students to tell what they think their community leaders could do to solve the problem. Lead students to the idea that they must come up with several possible solutions, such as changing an open field that the town owns to a playing field; buying land to make a playing field; or turning conservation land into a playing field. Write the steps in the problem-solving process so far: *1) Name the problem. 2) Come up with several possible solutions.* Then ask students to say how they feel about the three possible solutions to the playing field problem. Some, for example, may say that the town should never give up its conservation land. When students give an opinion on one of the possible solutions, tell them that they are evaluating, or making a judgment about, the possible solution. Record this as step three in the process of solving problems: *3) Evaluate the possible solutions.* Explain that problem solvers must look closely at all the possible solutions to determine what they think is good or bad about them. After careful evaluation, the last step in the problem-solving process takes place: *4) Choose a solution.* Project *Solutions Master 12: Flowchart.* Label the four boxes

Solutions Master 12: Flowchart

with the steps in the process of solving problems. Review how you would complete the chart using the sample problem you just explored.

Practice the Skill Distribute copies of *Solutions Master 12: Flowchart* to students. Have students write the steps in the problem-solving process above the four boxes. Then present a problem that is suggested by the topic you are currently teaching. For example, students might look at the problem of water as a limited resource through the lens of their own town, neighborhood, school, or home. Ask pairs of students to use the problem-solving process to suggest the best solution that they, as individuals and schoolchildren, could actually carry out. Leave the completed example on *Solutions Master 12: Flowchart* on display as students work through the process. Review students' completed flowcharts and solutions.

Support a Position

To support a position, students give information that explains, develops, or provides examples and other evidence in order to prove a point. Students must develop this skill in order to write well-developed paragraphs. They also need this skill in order to speak persuasively. Learning to support a position is also important in helping students learn how to elaborate, or say more about a topic.

Teach the Skill Project *Solutions Master 13: Support Chart*. In the top box, write an opinion statement related to a topic you are teaching, such as this one: *Ben Franklin was a great scientist* (Grade 3, Grade 5). Tell students that this is an opinion or position statement: it tells how the writer feels about Ben Franklin. Ask students to tell you what the writer needs to do to convince the reader or listener that this idea is true. Guide students to see that the writer needs to tell ways in which Ben Franklin was a great scientist, or what he did in terms of science that made him great. That is, the author or speaker needs to elaborate or add support. Note that support consists of any details that prove or develop the main idea or opinion. Write and read supporting statements such as the following:

Solutions Master 13:
Support Chart

> *Ben Franklin invented a stove that was a safe way to heat houses.*
> *Ben Franklin invented a new kind of eyeglasses that people still*
>   *use today.*
> *Ben Franklin helped people understand electricity.*

Record the statements in the Support Chart below the opinion. Review what the completed chart shows, and note how much more persuasive the opinion becomes when there is support to explain and back it up.

Practice the Skill Present a textbook example of support. For example, point out one or more paragraphs that tell why the quilts of Gee's Bend are so special (Grade 4, page 101). Have students identify the support for this opinion. For additional practice, distribute copies of *Solutions Master 13: Support Chart*, and have students generate support for an idea based on a topic you have studied recently. For example, write this opinion: *Schools are the most important public service in our community* (based on Grade 3). Have students support the position by using what they have learned, by referring back to the textbook, and/or by working with a partner to come up with new ideas.

Distinguish Fact and Opinion

When students separate facts and opinions, they begin by analyzing what they read and hear in order to separate what is true, or able to be verified or proven, from what is believed, felt, or judged. Practice with this skill helps students become more critical readers and listeners.

Teach the Skill Begin with students' ideas about the difference between a fact and an opinion to elicit the idea that a fact is often a date, a statistic, or other record of events that they can look up to be sure it is true. On the other hand, an opinion expresses beliefs or feelings about a subject. Students cannot look opinions up in a reference source to be sure that they are true. In addition, opinions are sometimes stated using clue words, such as *think, believe,* or *feel,* that suggest the ideas presented are not certain. Opinions also sometimes include describing words that show the writer's judgment of the subject; for example, they may use the words *best, worst, good, okay, bad, lucky, great, most,* and so on. Write some facts and opinions about a topic under study. Include clue words in some, but not in all. For example, write:

> *Making maps is an interesting job.*
> *I feel that economists are the most important social scientists.*
> *An economist uses data, such as the prices of items, in his or her work.*

Have students tell which statements they think are opinions and which are facts. Project *Solutions Master 3: Two-Column Chart,* label the columns *Fact* and *Opinion,* and record students' ideas. Review why each statement is a fact or opinion. Circle the clue words *feel* and *most important* in the opinion.

Practice the Skill Give students written text that includes both fact and opinion statements, such as the following, on any topic under study:

> *Ben Franklin was born in 1706.*
> *Ben Franklin was the greatest founder of our country.*
> *Ben Franklin wrote funny newspaper stories.*
> *Ben Franklin moved to Philadelphia.*
> *Ben Franklin was a great scientist.*
> *Ben Franklin was lucky at business.*
> *Ben Franklin helped Philadelphia become the greatest city in America.*
> *Ben Franklin helped write the Declaration of Independence.*
> *I think that the United States became independent because of Ben Franklin.*
> *Ben Franklin died in 1790.*

Ask students to look for characteristics that will help them decide if the statements are facts or opinions. Remind them that statements of fact can be proven true. Opinions are statements that express a person's belief or feeling. Distribute copies of *Solutions Master 3: Two-Column Chart,* have students label the headings *Fact* and *Opinion,* and ask them to record the statements of fact and opinion in the correct column. In addition, have students circle any clue words that tell them the statements are opinions. Discuss their choices.

Solutions Master 3:
Two-Column Chart

Identify Point of View

When students determine point of view, they ask who is writing and why. They also examine what effect the identity of the author and the author's purpose have on the information conveyed. Identifying first-person point of view can be a first step in recognizing bias.

Teach the Skill As needed, begin with some background information and examples. Explain that point of view is the relationship of a person to his or her subject. For example, a person who is writing about global trade may have the point of view of someone who has lost his or her job as a result of global trade or someone who is now making a lot more money because of global trade. Sometimes, pronouns help reveal a person's attitude toward his or her subject. When a writer uses the first person, employing words such as *I, me, my, mine, we, us,* and *our,* the writing is often subjective and based more on personal experience and feelings than on broad experience or accepted facts. When a writer uses the third person, employing words such as *he, she, it, they, them* and never inserting himself or herself into the text, the writing may be objective; that is, it may be more factual or more universally accepted as true.

Present students with two examples of objective and subjective points of view on the same topic. For example, you might present textbook information about public transportation (Grade 3) in combination with selected or created copy from an editorial in a local newspaper complaining about the cost of public transportation or some other problem with it. Project *Solutions Master 3: Two-Column Chart,* and ask students to compare the writing in terms of who they think wrote each piece and what the author's purpose was in each case. Ask which writer seems more emotional or personally involved in the topic. Write the heading *Editorial* in the first column and write *personal* and/or *emotional* in the first cell. Ask which writer uses words such as *I, me, my, mine, we, us,* and *our,* and write the specific pronouns used in the left column. Note that the writer perhaps uses public transportation every day, or wants to use it more but cannot. He or she is personally close to the subject. Write *close to subject* in the first column. Students might also decide that the editorial consists more of opinions than facts; if so, record the word *opinions* in the first column of the chart. Then label the second column *Textbook.* Guide students to discover some of the differences in point of view, such as the fact that the textbook is not emotional or personal, the writer does not use the pronouns *I, me, my, mine, we, us,* and *our;* the writer seems far away from the topic; and the writer is more concerned with presenting facts than with opinions or feelings. Record these ideas in the second column. Then explain that the information in the first column of the chart describes first-person point of view. Circle the information in the cells of the first column, write the label *First-Person Point of View,* and draw a linking line from the circle to the label. Do the same with the second column for third-person point of view.

Practice the Skill Find a first-person account for students to read. Ask them to identify clues to the point of view, such as the use of first-person pronouns; evidence of feelings or emotions; many opinions, or more opinions than facts; and information they infer about how close to the subject the writer is. Present a

Solutions Master 3:
Two-Column Chart

third-person treatment on a similar subject, and have students identify clues to point of view. Alternatively, use a textbook example such as copy about Luzena Stanley Wilson (Grade 5, page 13), which includes an example of first-person point of view within copy that is written from the third-person point of view.

Recognize Bias

When students learn to recognize bias, they begin to understand how writers and speakers can influence others by presenting information that is unfair, one sided, or written for a purpose that is not directly stated. To recognize bias, students must first determine the point of view from which the piece is written. They must also use other skills, such as making inferences and drawing conclusions, to uncover a hidden agenda.

Teach the Skill Explain to students that bias is a one-sided point of view. All people have biases. When we vote in an election for one candidate, that is our bias. Bias becomes a problem when it is covered up, or when a writer presents his or her views as if they are fair and objective when they are not. Offer this example: suppose a writer discusses two candidates, pretending to like both equally. But, in truth, the writer prefers one. Without saying this directly, the writer may make many more positive comments about the candidate he or she prefers. Bias can also be more obvious. Bias is often expressed through very negative or very positive statements. Biased views typically leave out facts that go against the writer's opinion. Finally, a biased view also often overstates or understates. The writer tries to make something bigger and better, or smaller and worse, than it really is. Project *Solutions Master 14: Recognize Bias Checklist* and review what it shows. Note that students should place a checkmark in the right-hand column for any question that can be answered yes. A completed organizer with one checkmark suggests there is a chance of bias. Completed organizers with two or more checkmarks suggests that there is probably bias.

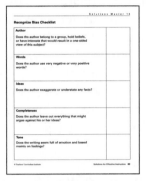

Solutions Master 14: Recognize Bias Checklist

Practice the Skill Distribute the passage below and read it with students. Tell them it is from a very early description of Louisiana that can be found on the Library of Congress Web site. Explain that it was written in 1720 by John Law, a man whose company controlled all the trade in Louisiana. Ask students to underline anything in the passage that they think shows bias. Then hand out copies of *Solutions Master 14: Recognize Bias Checklist*. Have students use the checklist to determine whether and/or in what ways the passage is biased. Review the completed checklists, requiring students to name their support for each checkmark they placed in the chart.

> *Corn, vines, and almost all the fruits of France grow there perfectly well. Tis one of the finest countries in the world, [filled] with gold, silver, copper, and lead mines. . . . There we will surely draw pieces of silver out of the earth. . . Soon we shall find healing remedies for most dangerous wounds. . . The wild bulls, of which there is great plenty, . . . the hair is very long, and like wool, only finer. There is a [great] number of deer and some bears that do no harm.*

Analyze Primary and Secondary Sources

An important part of the study of history is making judgments about and distinguishing between the sources we rely on to tell us what happened. When students make distinctions between sources, they begin to understand that some historical accounts are closer to or farther away from the truth than others are. They also begin to understand that a good historian must judge the worth of sources, as well as, often, put together many sources, before making statements about events, people, motives, and other aspects of history.

Teach the Skill Tell students that a primary source is information that comes from someone who lived during, took part in, or saw an event. List some types of primary sources, such as letters, diaries, and autobiographies. Tell students some primary source writers use words that tell the reader that they are expressing their own experience or point of view. These words include *I, me, my, mine,* and *myself,* as well as *we, us, our,* and *ourselves.* Primary source writers also often use vivid language that makes readers feel as though they are with the writer at the event. But not all primary sources are personal. A document such as the United States Constitution is a primary source, but it does include the word *our,* for example. It is not "up close and personal" either. Likewise, newspaper articles written at the time of the Civil War are primary sources about the Civil War, but these articles might not express a single personal feeling. In contrast, explain that secondary sources are written after an event takes place, sometimes hundreds of years later. They usually combine information from many sources, including primary sources. Explain that the textbook is a secondary source, although it may contain some primary sources such as photographs and documents from a certain time period. Other secondary sources include biographies that were not written when the subject was still alive and history books.

Project *Solutions Master 3: Two-Column Chart,* and label the headings *Primary Source* and *Secondary Source.* Display short excerpts from both primary and secondary sources on a topic you are teaching now, or use these sentences about westward expansion (Grade 5), and tell students that each one came from a different source:

Solutions Master 3:
Two-Column Chart

> *We rode in a wagon over muddy roads.*
> *The settlers traveled in rain and snow.*
> *I missed my friends back home in St. Louis.*
> *For us, the most dangerous time was winter.*
> *My brother seemed never to get warm that winter.*
> *No one is certain how many families took the trip West.*
> *We joined a long train of wagons.*
> *Our cow was tied to the wagon.*
> *Jimmy Smith roped the calf.*
> *The men and women who traveled the Oregon Trail experienced*
>   *many hardships.*

Ask students to identify the probable source of each statement as primary or secondary, and give a reason for their answers. (Some statements could be placed in both categories.) Record their answers, and use the completed graphic organizer to review some of the characteristics of each type of source.

Another way to approach the concept of point of view, as well as to teach primary and secondary sources, is to assign students to small groups and distribute a copy of *Solutions Master 7: Timeline/Judgment Graphic* to each group. Have students use the organizer as a continuum, labeling one end *True* and the other end *Not As True*. Ask students to work as group to rank sources such as diaries, biographies, autobiographies, newspaper accounts, and textbooks and place them on the continuum or judgment graphic. Encourage a variety of ideas and opinions about the meaning of *true*. For example, a person who witnessed an event may have the truest idea of it—or not. If a person was at a march with Dr. Martin Luther King, Jr., he or she knows what the march was like, or the small part of it he or she witnessed, but is not an expert on Martin Luther King, Jr., and is probably not an expert on the march either. Yet, he or she knows things firsthand that people who were not there do not know. Note that this person's account is a primary source. Review that primary sources are written by people who were at the events or lived at the time that the events were taking place. All other sources, such as the words in a textbook or history book that appeared later, are secondary sources, because they were written by people who did not witness the events. Use discussions about the sources on the continuum to reinforce the idea that different sources have different weaknesses and strengths.

Practice the Skill Give students a primary source on a topic you are studying or have studied as a class, such as a photograph of Clara Barton, as well as a secondary source on the same topic, such as the textbook or another account of Clara Barton. Divide the class into small groups and have them come up with one or more reasons why a primary source could be a good source of information and also why a secondary source could be a good source of information. Then ask them to come up with one way in which each type of source is limited, or lacks something that the other has. Have each group present its ideas, and use them to discuss the strengths and weaknesses of each type of source.

Solutions Master 7:
Timeline/Judgment Graphic

Graphic and Visual Skills: Read Graphs

A graph is a visual representation of data that shows a relationship between two or more things that can change. Some graphs show trends or changes over time.

Teach the Skill Introduce or review the following types of graphs: picture graphs, pie charts, bar graphs, and line graphs. Ask students to tell you what they already know about reading graphs. Have students turn to a graph in their textbooks (such as Grade 4, page 37), or have them focus on a classroom graph. Explain or review that no matter what type of graph students are looking at, they should always begin by reading the title; point out that the title often sums up the content and purpose of the graph. Their next step is to study the key, if there is one, so that they will know what each picture, symbol, or color on the graph stands for. Explain that not all graphs have a key, however, and sometimes students' next step will be to read the axes of the graph. Students should read any titles on the axes, as well as the units of measure provided. Then they can concentrate on interpreting each line or bar. That is, students should determine what the point on a line graph or bar on a bar graph shows, and how it is different from other points on the line or other bars. Finally, students should summarize what the graph shows. They may do this silently, orally with a partner, or in writing. A summary should begin with the title of the graph, a paraphrase of the title, or a statement based on the title telling what the graph shows.

Practice the Skill Have students study a different graph (such as the line graph on page 193 of Grade 4). With a small group, have them follow these steps: *1) Read the title. 2) Study the key. 3) Read the axes. 4) Interpret each line or bar. 5) Summarize.* Call for volunteers from different groups to report their summaries.

Graphic and Visual Skills: Read Flowcharts

All charts organize information. They also put the information into a visual format that usually summarizes the information or makes it simpler to understand or grasp. A flowchart categorizes information into steps in a process. Readers follow arrows to understand the progress or development over time of an activity or an event.

Teach the Skill Ask students to tell you how reading a chart is the same or different from reading a graph. Be sure to reinforce or elicit ideas about the importance of reading the title as well as any headings in order to get a clear overview of the purpose of the chart and what it shows. Explain that a flowchart is a special kind of chart that shows steps in a process or a sequence of events. Project *Solutions Master 12: Flowchart* to reacquaint students with the look of a flowchart, and explain that students should begin reading a flowchart by focusing on the box that is closest to the top, farthest to the left, or both. Then they should follow the arrows to read separate steps in a process in the order in which they should be performed or events in the order in which they occurred.

Practice the Skill Have students focus on a flowchart displayed in your classroom or a flowchart in one of their textbooks (such as the one shown in Grade 4 on pages 270–271). Ask them to identify what the flowchart shows by reading or paraphrasing the title. Then have them identify the separate steps in the process or events in a sequence of events.

Graphic and Visual Skills: Use Tables

Tables are like charts in that they display information in columns, but instead of displaying information in words, as most charts do, tables usually display data in both columns and rows. Tables make excellent reference tools, because users can refer to them to find specific information at a glance.

Teach the Skill Use an example from the textbook (such as Grade 4, page 219); create a table using *Solutions Master 5: Three-Column Chart;* or present another

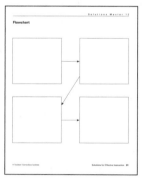

Solutions Master 12: Flowchart

Solutions Master 5:
Three-Column Chart

example of a table to show students what tables look like and how they display information. If needed, review the terms *column* and *row*. Explain that students should always begin studying a table by reading the title and then reading the headings, which often appear not only at the top of columns but also at the beginning of rows. Have students practice reading the table you are presenting as an example by naming or summarizing this information. Then ask students to find and name specific bits of information that the table includes. For example, if using the table at Grade 4, ask them to identify the average July temperature in San José. After students name it, ask them to compare it to the average January temperature in Las Vegas. Have students tell you how they found each bit of information, and review reading both across the rows and down the columns to find target information. Also, invite students to summarize what the table shows.

Practice the Skill Challenge pairs or teams of students to construct a table. Have them use it to display data about a topic under study, such as the Midwest. For example, students might make a table that shows the states of the Midwest with data about each state's rank in population or area, which they can locate using online sources. Students can create their tables by using copies of *Solutions Master 5: Three-Column Chart,* word-processing their tables, or using a ruler and/or lined paper to construct them. Remind students to create clear headings for their tables. When students have completed their tables, invite them to exchange their tables with other pairs or groups, and to use the tables to locate specific bits of data.

Graphic and Visual Skills: Use Webs

Web diagrams, which are also called concept webs, cluster diagrams, and wheel and spoke diagrams, help students organize or arrange details around a central opinion, focus, topic, or main idea. Using web diagrams provides excellent practice in analysis and can be used to identify or generate an opinion and reasons, a main idea and details, or a class and its members. In all of these ways, using a web helps students see how ideas relate to one another and to a larger concept. Students can make their own webs to develop, demonstrate, or communicate their understanding of a topic. The skill is applicable to all areas of social studies.

Teach the Skill Project *Solutions Master 10: Web,* and ask students how they would use it to show what they have learned about a topic you have recently studied as a class. For example, to review interesting places in the United States and the students' geographical relationship to them (Grade 3), you might ask, *Say we wanted to use this web to show where our town or city is in the United States. What would I write in the center?* Record the best answer. Then ask for students' ideas about what to write in the secondary circles, such as *east of the Golden Gate Bridge.* Have students summarize what the web shows.

Practice the Skill Group students in pairs, and distribute copies of *Solutions Master 10: Web* to each pair, or ask students to draw their own webs. Have them use their web to show what they have learned about a recent topic under study (such as the peoples of the United States, Grade 4). Discuss the completed webs. If you wish, extend teaching to review the skill of analysis, which students have

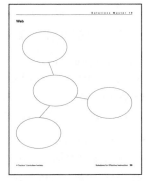

Solutions Master 10: Web

just used to create the web; to review classification; or to teach expository paragraph construction from a web by using it to generate a topic sentence and supporting information.

Graphic and Visual Skills: Analyze Timelines

The ability to analyze a timeline is crucial to the study of history. Timelines enable students to view time periods as a series of chronological events. Like charts, timelines summarize and simplify information. They provide a kind of brief, chronological outline rather than an in-depth discussion.

Teach the Skill Present a timeline to your students (such as the timeline in Grade 5, page 277), or construct a simple timeline using *Solutions Master 7: Timeline/Judgment Graphic*. Ask students to tell what the timeline shows, reminding them, as needed, always to begin analyzing any chart, table, graph, or other organizer by reading the title and getting an overview in that way. If there is a caption, this may also aid them in the process of summing up what the timeline shows; however, captions sometimes add new information or comment on specific details in the timeline. Explain that the next step in the process of analyzing a timeline is to determine the time span it shows, if this information is not already given in the title. For example, a timeline may show the years 1790 through 2000. After determining the topic and the time span, students should also look at the intervals, that is, the length of time between the marks that show dates on the timeline. This helps them develop a sense of how slowly or rapidly events occurred over time. Next, students should read the individual dates and labels, as well as study any illustrations if they are present. A final step in analyzing a timeline is to sum up—orally, silently, or in writing—what the timeline shows.

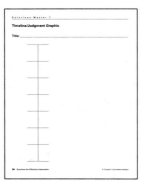

Solutions Master 7:
Timeline/Judgment Graphic

Practice the Skill Point out or project a different timeline. Ask one student to tell you the first step in analyzing the timeline, and have another student perform it. Continue with all the steps in the process of analyzing a timeline, including the final step of summarizing.

Graphic and Visual Skills:
Analyze Photographs and Other Images

Students can learn about history by analyzing photographs, illustrations, and other images. Sometimes, visual information can express ideas or emotions that the text alone does not convey. Sometimes, visual information also adds to what the text says or presents a slightly different angle on it.

Teach the Skill Display a photo from the text that is rich for analysis, such as the photo that shows a school closing as a result of the chemicals in a nearby canal (Grade 3, page 81). Ask, *What is going on in the picture?* Encourage your students to give as much detail as possible, as well as to distinguish between what seems most important and what seems less or least important. Note that occasionally, a visual will have a title; usually, it will have a caption. Ask students to identify these elements, if present, and explain what they tell. Explain that in addition to analyzing photographs, good critical thinkers make judgments about them. That is because photographs and other illustrations can be used to express a point of view, and they can also contain bias. While it is usually true that a photograph does not lie (unless digitally manipulated), a photographer still makes a choice when deciding what to show about a subject, what to include in the foreground, what to put in or leave out of the background, and so on. Challenge students to make judgments or inferences based on the photograph you are showing to them. Then have students name the steps in the process of analyzing photographs or other images: *1) Determine what is going on, including what is most or least important. 2) Read the title and caption, if present. 3) Make inferences and/or judgments about the choices made by the photographer or other artist.*

Practice the Skill Have pairs of students select a photograph from a chapter of the textbook that they have recently studied and use the process above to analyze it. Have pairs share their photograph and analysis with other pairs. When both pairs reach a consensus about what each photograph shows, have them present their analysies to the class.

Part Two

Integrating Language Arts Strategies

Prereading Strategies

Preview and Predict Content

Have students preview each chapter to determine its subject, major topics, new vocabulary, and length. Then have students use this information in combination with text illustrations to predict what they will learn.

Variation Have students read a selected portion of text and predict what will happen next or what will be explained or introduced next. Ask students to justify and discuss their predictions by asking them questions such as, *Why do you think so?* and/or *What part of the text gave you that clue?* Then record the predictions on the board or on a transparency. Have students read another segment of the text, searching for information that confirms or disproves their predictions. Guide them to revise or confirm their predictions. Revise the transparency as needed.

Identify Chapter Structure

Have students work in pairs to identify the organizational plan of a chapter. Distribute *Solutions Master 15: Beginning-Middle-End Chart,* and have students list the parts of the chapter that belong in each part.

Variation Identify the chapter parts and features, such as the title, introductory text, section heads, vocabulary, section text, summary, illustrations, captions, page numbers, and Reading Further, and have students write them in the correct column of the Beginning-Middle-End chart. Note that some elements should appear in more than one column.

Conduct a Chapter Features Scavenger Hunt

Have students conduct a "scavenger hunt" for section heads, visuals, captions, vocabulary, and other chapter features. Distribute *Solutions Master 16: Chapter Features Chart.* If needed, review the different types of chapter features with a class, and then ask students to locate one example to write in the middle column. Then have students locate at least one example of each text feature in the rest of the chapter. Review results as a class. Ask if there are additional features that the chart does not name. (For example, there is a focus question at the beginning of the chapter, and, at grades 4 and 5, the Reading Further head is followed by a focus statement or two in heavy black type.)

Solutions Master 15: Beginning-Middle-End Chart

Solutions Master 16: Chapter Features Chart

Link Chapter Parts to Book Parts

Write the chapter title, one social studies vocabulary word, and one key concept on the board. Ask where, besides in the chapter itself, students can find each of these elements. Review the purposes and use of the Table of Contents, glossary, and index as needed.

Predict Pattern of Organization

Have students use the chapter title, headings, and illustrations to predict chapter order. For example, they may predict chronological or sequential order. They may also predict organization by main idea and details, cause and effect, comparison and contrast, problem and solution, or other expository methods. (Note that some chapters have more than one method of organization.)

Optional Extension Have students revise and confirm their predictions about the methods of organization during and after reading.

Use a KWL Chart

Have students preview the chapter. Hand out *Solutions Master 17: KWL Chart,* and have students complete the first two columns. Alternatively, project the chart as a transparency and complete the first two columns as a class.

Solutions Master 17:
KWL Chart

Create an Anticipation Guide

Prepare three or four statements based on chapter content. Write them on the board or hand them out, and read them aloud.

Example *It is more important to recycle items than it is to reuse them.*

Ask students to agree or disagree with each statement, or ask students to say *true* or *false*. Restate and/or record the class consensus.

Model the Guiding Questions Strategy

Turn the first subhead title into a question. Ask students to read to find the answer. Encourage students to use this strategy on their own as they read.

During Reading Strategies

Model the "Talk Back" Strategy

Tell students that it's a great idea to talk back—aloud, if they are alone, or silently—when they read. To model this strategy, read the first section of the chapter and then produce a short summary that begins, *This section tells me that . . .* or *I learned that . . .* Group students in pairs and ask them to continue using this strategy as they read.

Variations Students can also question, react to interesting information, or tell what confuses them.

Provide Tips for Note Taking

1. Photocopy one section of the chapter and project it as a transparency.

2. Read the section aloud as students follow along. Ask them to react by telling you what's important, what's new, or what is hard to understand. Or ask them to tell you what they can see in their mind's eye as they read the text.

3. Model methods of taking notes based on students' answers.

   - **Use sticky notes.** Show how you might write * on a sticky note to place next to a main idea, ! on a sticky note to place next to something surprising, or ? on a sticky note to place next to something confusing.
   - **Use graphic organizers.** Show how you might sketch your own support chart, main idea and details web, or other organizer to record information.
   - **Sketch.** Show how you might make simple sketches or diagrams to help you understand and remember ideas as you read.

Use the Make Connections Chart

Distribute copies of *Solutions Master 18: Make Connections Chart* or project it as a transparency. Help students list chapter content and make connections to their own life. For example, students might link the concept of being diverse to their own classroom or neighborhood, or to the range of first and last names of their friends and acquaintances.

Solutions Master 18:
Make Connections Chart

Reinforce Sequencing Skills

For chapters that are organized by chronological or sequential order, have students identify what happens first (or what to do first), next, and so on. Distribute copies of *Solutions Master 6: Sequence Chain* and have students work in pairs to record chronological order or steps in a process. Depending on chapter content, explain that students may need to add more boxes or that they may not fill in every box. For chapters where constructing a timeline may be the best way to show chronological or sequential order, distribute copies of *Solutions Master 7: Timeline/Judgment Graphic*.

Variation When a chapter lists many events or steps in a process, it might be possible for small groups of students to form a human flowchart, sequence chain, or timeline. Each student pair or small group of students should hold a sheet of paper with one event or step written clearly in big letters and line up in order.

Analyze Cause and Effect

For chapters that include a single cause and effect, a single cause and multiple effects, or a single effect with multiple causes, display *Solutions Master 1: Cause-and-Effect Diagram* and model how you would label the boxes, as well as how you might not use all the boxes or add some boxes. Then distribute copies of *Solutions Master 1: Cause-and-Effect Diagram* for students to complete.

Analyze a Sequence of Causes and Effects

For chapters that include a chain of causes and effects, display *Solutions Master 2: Cause-and-Effect Chain* and model how you would fill in the first cause and effect. Note, also, how you might not use all the boxes or add some boxes. Then distribute copies of *Solutions Master 2: Cause-and-Effect Chain* for students to complete.

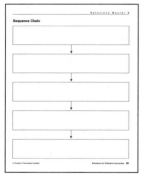

Solutions Master 6:
Sequence Chain

Solutions Master 7:
Timeline/Judgment Graphic

Solutions Master 1:
Cause-and-Effect Diagram

Solutions Master 2:
Cause-and-Effect Chain

Use a Diagram to Compare and Contrast

For chapters that include both significant comparisons and contrasts, distribute copies of *Solutions Master 4: Venn Diagram*, or project it as a transparency. Work as a class to create a title for the Venn diagram. Review what to write in each part of the diagram. Have students complete the diagram individually or in pairs.

Use Charts to Compare or Contrast

For chapters that present comparisons or contrasts, distribute copies of either *Solutions Master 3: Two-Column Chart* or *Solutions Master 5: Three-Column Chart,* or project it as a transparency. Work as a class to create a title for the chart and the column headings. Then complete the chart as a class, or have students complete the chart individually or in pairs.

Identify Facts and Opinions

For chapters that mingle fact and opinion, distribute copies of *Solutions Master 3: Two-Column Chart*. Have students use the chapter title to create a heading for their chart. Have them label the columns *Fact* and *Opinion* and complete the chart individually or in pairs.

Make Inferences/Draw Conclusions

Project a copy of *Solutions Master 8: Inference/Conclusion Diagram* and model how you would use it to make inferences or draw conclusions as you read. For inferences, label the top boxes *Fact or Idea* and *What I Already Know*. Label the bottom rectangle *Inference*, and using an example from the text, model how you would draw an inference and record your thinking process. For a conclusion, label the top *Facts*, or write *Text Information* and *More Text Information*. Label the bottom rectangle *Conclusion*, and using two or more ideas from the text, model how you would draw a conclusion and record your thinking process.

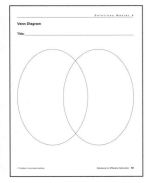

Solutions Master 4:
Venn Diagram

Solutions Masters 3:
Two-Column Chart

Solutions Masters 5:
Three-Column Chart

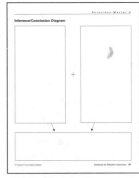

Solutions Master 8:
Inference/Conclusion Diagram

Identify Narrative Information

For chapters that retell events, distribute copies of *Solutions Master 19: 5W and H Chart,* or project it as a transparency. Work as a class to create a title for the chart. Have students complete the chart individually or in pairs.

Create a Web of the Main Idea and Details

Project or distribute *Solutions Master 10: Web.* Explain that, usually, a chapter section presents at least one main idea. Help students identify the main idea of a section and record it in the center of the web. Then have students identify the details that tell about or explain the main idea and record them in the secondary circles.

Variation Use *Solutions Master 10: Web* with individual paragraphs or with the chapter as a whole.

Create a Chart of the Main Idea and Details

Project *Solutions Master 13: Support Chart.* Explain that, usually, a chapter section presents one main idea. Help students identify the main idea of a section and record it in the first row of the chart. Then have students identify the details that tell about or explain the main idea and record them.

Variations

- Use *Solutions Master 13: Support Chart* as a basis for teaching summarizing. Have students identify what belongs in a summary and what doesn't.

- Use *Solutions Master 13: Support Chart* with individual paragraphs or with the chapter as a whole.

Apply Main Idea and Details Learning

Photocopy one section of a chapter. Cut it into parts that include the main idea and details or other explanation. Have students work in pairs to identify the parts and put the parts back together in correct order.

Optional Extension Have students glue the parts in order onto sheets of paper. Ask them to say the name of or label each part as the main idea or details.

State and Categorize Learning

Help students identify main ideas by contributing to a class chart. First, create a poster or chart titled *What I Learned Today About . . .* and have a volunteer complete that with a word or phrase that sums up the chapter content. Then have each student write a response on a sticky note and put it on the class chart. Review the results as a class. Remove duplicates. Then challenge students to sort notes into main ideas and details.

Solutions Master 19:
5W and H Chart

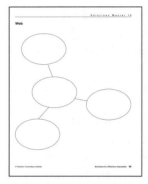

Solutions Master 10: Web

Solutions Master 13:
Support Chart

After Reading Strategies

Use a KWL Chart
Return to the *Solutions Master 17: KWL Chart*, and have students complete the last column.

Return to the Anticipation Guide
If there is a strong pedagogical purpose for doing so, such as a common misconception about chapter content that surfaced during prereading, return to and discuss the statements that students responded to before reading the chapter.

Find Answers in the Text
Pose recall questions and have students point to or use a sticky note to identify the exact place in the text where the answers are found.

Use Physical Categorization
Have students physically categorize information such as landforms, regions, natural resources, or other categories by assuming the identity of one member of a category, such as mesas, and then going to a designated part of the room where landforms of the West and Southwest gather.

Sum It Up
Have students use section heads to sum up the content of each section.

Return to Reading Graphic Organizers
Have students use any graphic organizers they filled in during reading to summarize chapter or section content or to identify gaps in their knowledge, problems, or questions.

Summarize 3-2-1
Have students summarize chapter content by stating the following:

- 3 new things they found out
- 2 interesting things they learned
- 1 question they still have

Create a Hand Summary
Have students trace the outline of their hand on a piece of paper. Tell them to write the subject or main idea of the chapter or of the Reading Further segment inside the outline of the thumb. Have them use the fingers to list details that help tell about, illustrate, or explain the subject or main idea.

Create Exit Slips
Have students write an "Exit Slip" by having them freewrite for five minutes on what they learned from the chapter. Students do not need to worry about order or organization in this exercise but should instead strive to record all the main ideas and details they can recall.

Solutions Master 17:
KWL Chart

Reflect

Have students reflect on the following:

- things they learned
- ways they learned
- strategies they can use to learn when they study the next chapter

Vocabulary Development Strategies

Rate Word Knowledge

Distribute *Solutions Master 20: Word Knowledge Chart*, and have students complete it on their own using new chapter vocabulary. In most cases, tell students they will not fill all the rows of the chart. In a few cases, they will need to add rows.

Use Syllabication in the Decoding Process

Write chapter social studies words of three or more syllables. Draw lines between the syllables. Point to the letters that represent the sounds as you slowly say each syllable. Then say the words slowly again and have students repeat them.

Identify Affixes and Roots

Write the social studies words. Have students identify familiar prefixes, suffixes, base words, or roots. Have them name other words that share the same word part.

Example government—environment, shipment, placement, fragment

Variation Write the social studies word but leave blanks for key word parts, such as a prefix, base, root, or suffix. Have students supply the word part.

Keep a Word Parts Log

Project *Solutions Master 21: Word Parts Log*. Show how you would record a word such as *prejudiced* in the top part of the log because it has the familiar prefix *pre-*. Then ask students for the meaning of the word, relate it to the meanings of other words with the same prefix, record the meaning, and talk about how the familiar word parts help you understand the word. Distribute copies of the Solutions Master and ask students to keep their own log of familiar word parts.

Use a Web for Structural Analysis

For words with word parts that students can use to make useful generalizations to other words, project *Solutions Master 10: Web*. Write one social studies word in the center of the web. Have students name other words with the same word part and record them.

Example renewable—redo, rewrite, rethink, revising

Develop Word Families

Write each social studies vocabulary word. Have students name words in the same family. List the words.

Example economy—economics, economist, economical

Variation Use *Solutions Master 10: Web* to lead the class in this activity or to provide a framework or organizing structure for students to use on their own.

Present Cognates

Help Spanish-speaking students make connections by presenting the following cognates as they learn each related social studies word:

Solutions Master 20:
Word Knowledge Chart

Solutions Master 21:
Word Parts Log

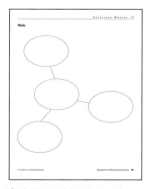

Solutions Master 10:
Web

Grade 3 *geografía, esfera (sphere), hemisferio, primer meridiano, océano, continente, estado (state), dirección cardinal, cañón, tradición, símbolo, geografía física, clima, recursos naturales, región, inmigrante, discriminar, diverso, cultura, boicot, canal, voluntario, mercado, economía, servicios, demanda, suburbia, candidato, polución, recursos renovables (renewable resources), communidad global, hábitat, tolerante*

Grade 4 *especialista en ciencias sociales (social scientist), ciencia social, economista, politólogo (political scientist), historiador, arqueólogo, escala, cultura, diverso, colonia, inmigrante, democracia, pico (peak), Revolución norteamericana, canal, producción masiva, polución, sabana, huracán, mineral, delta, petroleo, plantación, segregación, navegable, industria, agricultura, tornado, fértil, frontera, autosuficiente, fertilizante, pesticida, maíz, recurso renovable (renewable resource), mesa, desierto, adaptar, acueducto, cañón, cueva, caverna, misión, rebelión, capital, tributario, río, irrigación, hábitat, conservación, paso, expedición, géiser, tecnología, mormón, geografía física, geografía humana, archivos, legislatura, servicios, mercado*

Grade 5 *geografía, clima, globo, latitud, longitud, istmo, migrar, migración, recursos naturales (natural resources), cultura, región, artefacto, mesa, gobierno (government), explorador, las Indias del Este, colonia, colono, democrático, aliado (ally), economia, industria, plantación, asamblea, aprendiz (apprentice), trata de esclavos, dilemma, esptiritual, capitolio, política, real, colonia, protesta, proclamación, Parlamento, delegado, importar, masacre, boicot, independencia, neutral, traidor, tirano, resolución, milicia, igualdad (equality), revolucer, estrategia, voluntario, alistar (enlist), mercenario, tratado (treaty), constitución, compromiso, gabinete, monarquía, república, enmienda (amendment), ratificar, prejuiciado, civil, territorio, anexar, adquisición, expedición, ceder, pionero, inmigrante, transcontinental, mormón, misionero, yugo (yoke), norte, abolicionista, tecnología, industrialización, segregación, refugiado*

Sort by Structure, Function, or Meaning

Have students sort social studies vocabulary into categories such as the following:

- one-syllable, two-syllable, and three-syllable words
- nouns, verbs, and adjectives or adverbs
- words and phrases
- words that are compound and not compound
- content categories, such as people and places, or people, places, and things
- proper nouns and common nouns (grades 4 and 5)

Hand out *Solutions Master 3: Two-Column Chart* or *Solutions Master 5: Three-Column Chart,* as appropriate. Have students work in pairs to label the columns and to list words in the correct column. Alternatively, project *Solutions Master 3: Two-Column Chart* or *Solutions Master 5: Three-Column Chart,* and work as a class to complete it.

Solutions Masters 3: Two-Column Chart

Solutions Masters 5: Three-Column Chart

Create Word Tiers

Use the social studies words to create word tiers that show levels of specificity. Project *Solutions Master 22: Word Tiers* or draw a tier on the board. Write the vocabulary word or term in the top box or tier. Place the word's definition in the second tier. Ask for examples or for more specific information about the term to record in the third tier.

Examples

Grade 3 Tier 1: *continent;* Tier 2: *one of the main landmasses of the world;* Tier 3: *Europe, Asia, Africa, North America, South America, Antarctica, Australia*

Grade 4 Tier 1: *minerals;* Tier 2: *natural substances found in rock;* Tier 3: *coal*

Grade 5 Tier 1: *artifacts;* Tier 2: *human-made objects that help us understand the people who made them and how they lived;* Tier 3: *pots, or pieces of pots; boxes for storing food*

Use a Word Web to Develop Meaning

For words that have synonyms and antonyms, as well as words that name categories, project *Solutions Master 23: Word Web.* Model how to complete it with a sample word or a review word. Then distribute copies of the word web, assign a social studies word, and have students work individually or in pairs to complete it.

Use a Word Map to Develop Meaning

For words that appear in the text with clear and easily recognizable context clues, as well as words that students can visually represent in some way, distribute copies of *Solutions Master 24: Word Map.* Have students work individually or in pairs to complete it.

Use a Word Wheel to Develop Meaning

Project *Solutions Master 25: Word Wheel.* Write a social studies word with a familiar word part in the middle of the circle. Label the outer segments of the circle *Kind of Word, Familiar Word Part,* and *Related Words.* (Or vary these labels as the words demand; for example, students might record syllables, synonyms, or words and phrases that the target word brings to mind.) Start by having the students identify whether the word is a naming word, action word, or describing word.

Solutions Master 22: Word Tiers

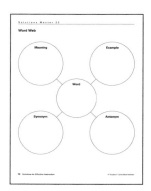

Solutions Master 23: Word Web

Solutions Master 24: Word Map

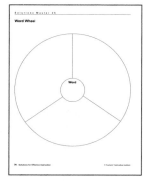

Solutions Master 25: Word Wheel

© Teachers' Curriculum Institute

Write their answer under *Kind of Word*. Then have students identify a familiar word part, such as the prefix *re-* or the suffix *-ion* or *-tion* and record it under *Familiar Word Part*. Finally, have students name words with one of the same word parts, and record them under *Related Words*.

Use Categories to Develop Meaning

Say and write a vocabulary word. Ask students to name a category it fits into.

Example Say *immigrant*. Students' answers might include the words *relatives, neighbors, leaders,* as well as the categories of three-syllable words, nouns or common nouns, and so on.

Variations

- Say and write a vocabulary word, such as *public services, primary sources,* or *suburbs*. Have students name words that belong in each category.
- Project *Solutions Master 25: Word Wheel*. Write the social studies word in the middle of the Word Wheel. Have students name examples that fit into the category and record them.

Solutions Master 25:
Word Wheel

Make Connections to the Meaning

Distribute copies of *Solutions Master 26: Word Connections Map*. Have students write the social studies word twice: once at the top of the page, and once in the upper left-hand box. Guide students to complete the organizer, or have them complete it in pairs or on their own by listing the other related social studies vocabulary words they learned with the new word; writing the chapter title, section title, or other description of the context in which they learned the word; speculating on ways to use the word; and coming up with their own method for remembering the word's meaning.

Solutions Master 26:
Word Connections Map

Make Word Ladders

Have students make word ladders. Word ladder options include adding one letter, changing one letter, deleting one letter, and anagramming.

Examples *peak—ape, pa; delta—deal, lad, ad*

Make Shorter Words from Longer Words

Have students make as many smaller words as they can from one longer word.

Make Word Crosses

Have students makes word crosses with the social studies vocabulary words. Students may use pen and paper, classroom letter cards, or letter tiles from a board game.

Play 10 Questions

Put students into groups and have each choose a social studies word from the current chapter or a word they have already learned. Then have them play a game of 10 Questions, posing questions such as, *Does it begin with a consonant? Does it have a* y *that sounds like a short* i*? Does it name places on the earth?*

Use Riddles

- Have students choose the hardest word and make up a rhyme, riddle, acronym, or other mnemonic for recalling it.
- Have students create word riddles by giving the clues one by one, such as, *It is made up of two words. Both words begin with the /f/ sound, but the first word is spelled with* ph. *It names things found on the earth.* Have a partner guess the word.

Optional Extension Have students make a book of social studies word riddles.

Play Tic-Tac-Toe

Have students play tic-tac-toe with social studies words and words that follow the same structural or phonemic patterns.

Examples

Grade 3 Player 1 writes *canal* in the middle and tries to make tic-tac-toe with other words that begin with the /k/ sound. Player 2 writes *state* and tries to make tic-tac-toe with other words that rhyme with *state*.

Grade 4 Player 1 writes *assembly line* in the middle and tries to make tic-tac-toe with phrases, while player 2 writes *plateau* and tries to make tic-tac-toe with words that have two syllables.

Grade 5 Player 1 writes *explorer* in the middle and tries to make tic-tac-toe with words that have the prefix *ex-*. Player 2 writes *revolution* and tries to make tic-tac-toe with words that end in *-tion*.

Present and Use Words in Context

Dictate sentences that use the words. Have students write the sentences. Then have students rewrite the sentences as questions.

Variations

- Dictate questions that use the words. Have students change the questions to statements. Or have students answer the questions using complete sentences.
- Dictate commands that use the words. Have students write the commands. Then have them change the commands to statements.
- Have pairs of students take turns dictating the words in declarative, interrogative, exclamatory, and imperative sentences.

Identify and Use Context Clues

Have students find unfamiliar words in the chapter. Then have students identify context clues and use them to help find the meaning, or part of the meaning, of the word. Review the types of context clues they find, such as restatements, definitions, synonyms, antonyms, and examples.

Variation Have pairs of students write sentences that use the social studies words and provide context clues for them.

Find Multiple Meanings

Elicit multiple meanings for words such as *scale* and *lock,* and provide cloze sentences and other oral and written contexts for students to use a variety of meanings in context.

Pair Social Studies and Academic Vocabulary

Write addition operations that include a high-frequency word and an academic vocabulary word. Challenge students to write or say a complete sentence that uses both words.

Example *explorers* + *discovered*—The explorers discovered a land they were not searching for.

Make an Illustrated Dictionary

Have students use sheets of paper, columns on a spreadsheet, separate word processing files, or index cards to make entries for an illustrated dictionary. After several lessons, have students alphabetize their entries and print out their spreadsheet, or put their entries into a word processing document or a booklet called "My Social Studies Dictionary."

Play a Matching Game

Create word cards with social studies vocabulary from several chapters, as well as other familiar words. Have students match activities and places, people and events, or other concept pairs that they create.

Examples

Matches for activity and place: agriculture + floodplain; settlement + Jamestown

Match for people and events: volunteers + natural disaster

Match for action or event and result: American Revolution + democracy

Generate Context

Use a social studies word to write or say a sentence about a picture in the text.

Variation Have students use a social studies word to write about something in their town or city.

Reinforce Spelling

Make word cards with social studies words that contain silent letters or silent letter patterns, such as -*igh*; unstressed syllables; and words that are commonly mispronounced because one or more of their sounds is elided, such as the first *n* in *government*. Write the words with these letters missing. Have pairs of students take turns drawing the cards and providing the missing letters.

Writing Process Overview Strategies

Present and Use a Writing Process Checklist

Distribute copies of either *Solutions Masters 27* or *28: Writing Process Checklist.* Review stages of the writing process and have students come up with new names for each, or provide terms that students might match with each stage, such as coming up with ideas, putting ideas on paper, making my writing better, and sharing writing.

Provide Frames and Steps for Creating Figures of Speech

As students revise letters, journals, stories, or other types of writing purposes and occasions that are appropriately enlivened by figurative language, provide frames for writing similes and metaphors.

Simile ____ is like ____ .

Metaphor ____ is ____ .

With the frames in view, remind students that similes and metaphors are fresh, new comparisons. To say a city is a crowded place is not a fresh, new comparison. It is just a comparison. To write a fresh new comparison, students need to follow these steps:

1 Think of your target word, such as *city*. Then think of a quality of a city. For example, a city is noisy.

2 Next, think of something that has that same quality. For example, a barking dog is noisy.

3 Write your simile: The city is like a barking dog.

4 Write your metaphor: The city is a barking dog.

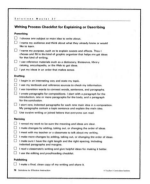

Solutions Master 27:
Writing Process Checklist

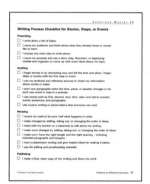

Solutions Master 28:
Writing Process Checklist

Create Writing Process Metaphors

Have students create metaphors for the writing process, such as, "Prewriting is a cheetah" (it speeds along); "Drafting is a tortoise" (it moves very slowly); "Publishing is songbird" (it is joyful; it communicates).

Set Up a Describing Words Round Robin

Write vocabulary words on cards, such as *cities, market, political scientist,* and *craftsmen.* Distribute several cards to small groups. Have each member of the group add one possible describing word to the card (such as *large, crowded; colorful, noisy; questioning, thoughtful; educated, talented; careful, successful*), and pass it along to the next person to add another. Continue around the group. Share the describing words as a class. Note how students can add describing words in the same way when they write.

Identify Topic Sentences

Have students identify the topic sentences of various paragraphs in their chapters. Have them explain the purpose of the topic sentence.

Variations

- If there are any paragraphs in the chapter that imply rather than state the topic sentence, have students work in pairs to write the topic sentence. Ask students to give explanations for why the topic sentence does not appear in the text.
- Photocopy a paragraph from the chapter that has a clear topic sentence, but block out the topic sentence. Distribute photocopies to the class. Have students write the topic sentence. Compare their version with the published version.

Use Visuals

Remind students that they can add visuals to their writing to help show ideas. Have students point out examples in the textbook of how photographs, illustrations, charts, graphs, maps, timelines, and other visuals work with the words to give information. Have students sketch visuals as part of the process of getting and organizing ideas during prewriting.

Use Software and Internet Resources

Encourage students to use appropriate software and the Internet at various stages of the writing process.

Prewriting Students can list, make spreadsheets, and use drawing tools. They may be able to access graphic organizers.

Writing Students can word-process; refer to dictionaries, thesauruses, and other tools that are part of their software or on the Internet; find or verify information online; and download free art for their writing, speaking presentations, and illustrated dictionaries.

Revising and Editing Students can use spelling and grammar checks, as long as they do not rely entirely upon them; use editing tools and second colors to highlight and revise; use various software options for graphs, charts, and other visuals; download pictures; insert headers, footers, and pagination; create covers; and revise and print out clean final copies.

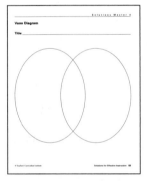

Solutions Master 4:
Venn Diagram

Develop Knowledge of Reference Materials

Have students find social studies terms, as applicable, in an online or print thesaurus, dictionary, atlas, or encyclopedia. Compare and contrast results of searches in various reference materials using *Solutions Master 4: Venn Diagram*, for example, for a dictionary and a thesaurus or *Solutions Master 3: Two-Column Chart* for an atlas and a dictionary. Elicit comparisons and contrasts of how the various materials are organized.

Solutions Master 3:
Two-Column Chart

Write Letters

Have students put themselves in a position of a historical character or a person living in a particular time and place in order to write a friendly letter, thank-you note, or invitation to another person living in the same era. Emphasize point of view, including the correct use of subject pronouns, as well as correct letter form, including punctuation of the date, salutation, and closing.

Prewriting Strategies

Get Ideas for Expository Writing

When the topic or writing purpose is open, have students brainstorm, list ideas, or freewrite to come up with ideas for writing. Model the process, noting how you select the best idea from your list after you have come up with several ideas.

Get and/or Organize Ideas for Narration

Hand out copies of *Solutions Master 6: Sequence Chain*. Have students use each box to record one event in a series of events or one step in a process. Note that students can add extra boxes on the back if they need them.

Variations Hand out copies of *Solutions Master 19: 5W and H Chart, Solutions Master 29: Story Map,* or *Solutions Master 15: Beginning-Middle-End Chart.* Show students how to use each organizer to jot down narrative ideas or parts.

Get and/or Organize Ideas for Presenting Cause and Effect

Project *Solutions Master 1: Cause-and-Effect Diagram.* Show students how to use the diagram to record one cause with one or more effects or one effect with one or more causes.

Solutions Master 6:
Sequence Chain

Solutions Master 19:
5W and H Chart

Solutions Master 29:
Story Map

Solutions Master 15:
Beginning-Middle-End Chart

Solutions Master 1:
Cause-and-Effect Diagram

Get and/or Organize Ideas for Presenting a Cause-and-Effect Chain

Project *Solutions Master 2: Cause-and-Effect Chain*. Show students how to use the diagram to record how a cause can lead to an effect that, in turn, leads to other causes or effects. Then distribute copies of the diagram for students to use in planning their own cause-and-effect chain analysis.

Get and/or Organize Ideas for Presenting Comparison and Contrast

Hand out copies of *Solutions Master 4: Venn Diagram*. Have students record their topic as a title and label the two outer circles with the names of the things they are comparing and contrasting. Instruct them to use the outer circles to write things that are different and the overlapping area to write things that are the same.

Get and/or Organize Ideas for Presenting Contrasts

Display *Solutions Master 3: Two-Column Chart* or *Solutions Master 5: Three-Column Chart*. Show students how to use each organizer to record their ideas about what they are contrasting. Then distribute the appropriate organizer for students to use on their own.

Get and/or Organize Ideas for Presenting Main Ideas and Details

Hand out copies of *Solutions Master 10: Web*.

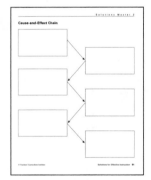

Solutions Master 2:
Cause-and-Effect Chain

Solutions Master 4:
Venn Diagram

Solutions Master 3:
Two-Column Chart

Solutions Master 5:
Three-Column Chart

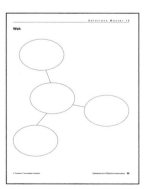

Solutions Master 10: Web

- If students are just beginning to prewrite, have them record their topic in the center of the web and other ideas in the outer circles.
- If students are at the organizing stage, have them write their topic in the center and main ideas for paragraphs in the outer circles.

Organize Ideas for Presenting Main Ideas and Details

Hand out copies of *Solutions Master 13: Support Chart.* Have students write their main idea at the top and details that explain or develop their main idea in the spaces marked *Support.*

Teach/Reinforce Expository Structure

When you assign compositions that explain or describe, project *Solutions Master 30: Composition Plan for Explaining or Describing.* Review the basic structure of expository writing, which includes an introduction, a body, and a conclusion. Then distribute copies of the master and ask students to use it to organize and draft their response.

Teach/Reinforce Persuasive Structure

When you assign compositions that persuade, project and distribute *Solutions Master 31: Composition Plan for Persuading.* Review the basic structure of persuasive writing, which includes an introduction, a body, and a conclusion, but which may sometimes lead up to the opinion statement instead of stating it directly in the first paragraph. Then distribute copies of the master and ask students to use it to organize and draft their response.

Use Note Cards

Help students who already have a central idea or clear opinion to prewrite, organize, and draft an expository or persuasive composition by using note cards. Distribute three or four note cards to each student. Explain that each note card represents a single body paragraph of their composition. Then have students write one main idea or reason for their opinion, as well as the details that explain, support, or develop it, on each note card. Explain that students may use two, three, or all of their note cards, depending on the number of body paragraphs they plan. Finally, ask students to put their cards in order. Using note cards you have developed for a sample expository or persuasive composition, model how you would turn each main idea or reason into a topic sentence and the details or other support into the remainder of the paragraph.

Solutions Master 13: Support Chart

Solutions Master 30: Composition Plan for Explaining or Describing

Solutions Master 31: Composition Plan for Persuading

Drafting Strategies

Move from Organizer to Draft

Demonstrate how to move from the graphic organizer to the draft. For example, display a completed Venn diagram. Point to the title and tell students that it is the subject of their composition or topic of their paragraph. Then note that the students' first sentence is about how the two things are alike, and point to the overlapping section of the Venn diagram. Then explain how their next sentence or sentences are about how the two things are different, and point to the outer parts of the Venn diagram. Model writing the draft from the organizer, making clear connections from organizer part to paragraph or composition part.

Present Sentence Starters

Write sentence starters on the board that are appropriate to the type of writing assigned. Model completing them.

Comparison
_____ and _____ are alike in many ways. First, both _____ and _____ . . .

Contrast
_____ and _____ are different in many ways. First, _____ . . . , but _____ . . .

Description
The _____ looks like . . . It has _____ . . . Sounds/Smells of _____ come from it.

Cause and Effect
First, _____ happened. That caused _____ . As a result, _____ . Because of _____ , . . .

Narration/Steps in a Process
First, _____ . Next/Second, _____ . Later/Then, _____ . Finally/Last/At last, _____ . . .

Main Ideas and Details/Persuasion
One reason for this is . . . An example of this is . . . That's why we should _____ now!

Identify Elements of Paragraphs

Have students follow along as you read aloud an expository paragraph from the lesson that has a clear topic sentence at the beginning, or project the paragraph on a transparency and read it aloud. Elicit the elements or characteristics of a paragraph by asking questions that compare it with shorter and longer units of discourse, a sentence and a composition. Help students identify both content and format characteristics, including a topic sentence that states a main idea, sentences that explain and support the main idea, transition words that link the sentences and that link the paragraph to other paragraphs, and the indented first sentence.

Variation/Extension Project *Solutions Master 4: Venn Diagram* and use it to compare and contrast a sentence and a paragraph or a paragraph and a composition.

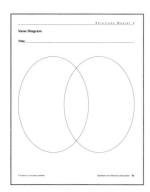

Solutions Master 4:
Venn Diagram

Create Visuals

To add information, interest, or clarity to their writing, encourage students to create or download copyright-free visuals such as charts and graphs to illustrate statistics; photos and illustrations to show people, places, and events; and time-lines or flowcharts to show an era, a sequence of events, or steps in a process. Encourage honest use of all information, and model how to write a source line.

Revising Strategies

Read Aloud

Have students read their work aloud to a classmate. Encourage them to listen for what sounds right and for the flow of ideas. Ask them to say what they do or do not understand or follow.

Engage in Peer Feedback

Have students work in pairs during the revision process. Project *Solutions Master 32: Peer Revising Checklist* and explain or elaborate on, as needed, each of the checklist items. Distribute a copy of the checklist to each student. Ask students to refer to it when engaging in the feedback process.

Add Describing Words

Before students revise, review describing words. Remind students that they tell color, size, shape, and other details about how things look. They also tell how things taste, smell, feel, or sound. Describing words can also tell how, how much or how many, when, and where. Model how you might add describing words to a sentence about, for example, foothills, a mesa, or a gorge, or to another sentence.

Solutions Master 32:
Peer Revising Checklist

Link Words with Visuals

If students have added visuals to their writing, have them ask themselves:

- Will my reader know why this picture/chart/other visual is here?
- Do I need a title?
- Do I need a caption?
- Do I need a sentence that introduces the visual?

Use an Editing and Proofreading Checklist

Distribute copies of *Solutions Master 33: Editing and Proofreading Checklist.* Teach or review checklist items as needed. Ask students to use the checklist to judge and change their writing.

Solutions Master 33:
Editing and Proofreading Checklist

Publishing Strategies

Create Covers
Encourage students to make covers that create interest in their work and also correctly telegraph the content of their writing. Use ideas for titles to review correct capitalization and punctuation of titles.

Create a Gallery Walk
Post or display writing assignments in the classroom. Give students time to walk around the room and read. Then, as a class, discuss students' reactions to the Gallery Walk.

Build a Portfolio
Have students create a folder, large envelope, notebook, or other holder for their work. Encourage students not only to file their writing here, but also to write comments on each piece of work they add to their portfolio. Comments can include things the student was proud of, found challenging, or hopes to improve the next time.

Optional Extensions
- Have students create a Table of Contents listing the pieces in their portfolio.
- Have students create a spreadsheet or list of pieces that links each work with a social studies concept, chapter, skill, or strategy. Students might also link their work with a pattern of organization (such as cause and effect or contrast), an audience, a purpose, or other aspects of writing that you are currently teaching or reinforcing, such as tone.
- Have students number the works in their portfolio. Then have them create an index of skills and strategies that tells which works reflect or use each.
- Have students keep an ongoing assessment in their portfolio detailing what they have learned via various assignments in terms of social studies content and/or in terms of becoming a better writer.
- Before sharing their portfolios, have students write a preface or introduction to their work with the intended audience in mind.

Make a Class Web Page
Create a Web site or add a page to your class Web site for social studies writing. (Your school IT professional may need to upload it to the net for you or link it to other school pages.) Use it to publish writing as well as to further a concrete sense of audience among your student writers.

Speaking and Listening Strategies

Give Precise Directions and Instructions

Have pairs of students use their completed copies of *Solutions Master 15: Beginning-Middle-End Chart* or *Solutions Master 16: Chapter Features Chart* to come up with exact instructions for using specific features, such as section headings, to increase their understanding of the text. Have pairs present their instructions and talk about what was most precise and useful in them.

Discuss New Words

Project *Solutions Master 20: Word Knowledge Chart,* and talk about how familiar students already are with new vocabulary terms. Invite students to talk about where they have heard the words before or what they think they mean. Use the chart to sum up the class's knowledge. Return to the chart to talk about how knowledge of the word has changed after students read the chapter and do the chapter activities.

Use a KWL Chart

Project *Solutions Master 17: KWL Chart,* and have students articulate what they know and what they want to learn about the topic they will read or hear about. After reading or listening, complete the chart by discussing and recording students' oral reflections.

Use Text Structure Graphic Organizers

1 Have students work together to summarize aloud the content of graphic organizers they used to take notes during reading or to generate and/or organize ideas for writing.

2 Have students complete graphic organizers such as a sequence chart, support chart, cause-and-effect diagram, or whatever is appropriate to the topic, as they listen to you read a section of the text aloud or as they listen to other oral reports or sources of information.

Solutions Master 15:
Beginning-Middle-End Chart

Solutions Master 16:
Chapter Features Chart

Solutions Master 20:
Word Knowledge Chart

Solutions Master 17:
KWL Chart

Connect with the Speaker

Distribute *Solutions Master 18: Make Connections Chart.* Have students fill it in before, during, or after they listen to connect and relate their own prior experiences, insights, and ideas with those of the speaker.

Provide a Beginning, Middle, and End

Distribute copies of *Solutions Master 15: Beginning-Middle-End Chart.* Have students use it as a planning guide for speaking when they are conveying information. Remind them that their beginning has to establish their purpose and create interest. Their middle has to express and develop their main idea, as well as stick to the topic. The end has to summarize briefly and leave the listener with a final powerful, amusing, or interesting thought.

Ask Thoughtful Questions

Remind students to ask thoughtful questions following their classmates' presentations. Before beginning presentations, have students brainstorm a set of guidelines that define thoughtful questions, as well as desirable behaviors related to asking questions. Engage in a think-aloud to help initiate the process. For example, you might say: *I love it when a listener raises his hand before asking a question.* Write *raise hand before speaking* on the board. Continue this process for a few minutes until you have generated about ten items. Post this list in a visible place or leave it on the board for the duration of the presentations.

"Read" Illustrations

Have students work together to summarize aloud what one or more of the chapter illustrations show. Encourage them to use social studies words and describing words.

Read-Pair-Share

1 Have students read sections of the chapter on their own.

2 Pair students. Have them discuss what they read in an open-ended way, or assign something to identify orally, such as a sequence, a category and its members, a main idea, or a cause and effect.

3 Have one member of the pair report to the class.

Paraphrase Oral Information

When you orally introduce or sum up a chapter or section, have students work in pairs to paraphrase what you said.

Variations

• When students give oral reports, have listeners paraphrase what they heard.

• When students act as each other's peer readers during the writing process, have the writer paraphrase the feedback given by his or her reader.

Solutions Master 18:
Make Connections Chart

Solutions Master 15:
Beginning-Middle-End Chart

Recite, Retell, Summarize, Paraphrase

Use Reading Further sections as opportunities to teach, model, and have children practice the oral skills of reciting, retelling, and paraphrasing.

Examples

Grade 3 Students can recite the names of explorers, retell what happened on October 12, 1492, or summarize the information in the chart on page 14.

Grade 4 Students can paraphrase "Life on the Mississippi Long Ago" on page 27, and recite the names of states along the Mississippi River.

Grade 5 Students can retell the story of Luzena Stanley Wilson on pages 12–15 and sum up the information shown by the map on page 13.

Optional Extension Have students use *Solutions Master 29: Story Map* or *Solutions Master19: 5W and H Chart* to help them plan before retelling a narrative. Have students use *Solutions Master 10: Web* or *Solutions Master13: Support Chart* to help them plan before paraphrasing or summarizing information in expository text.

Solutions Master 29: Story Map

Solutions Master 19: 5W and H Chart

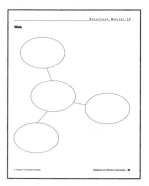
Solutions Master 10: Web

Solutions Master 13: Support Chart

Draw, Sketch, or Diagram Information

1 Encourage students to draw, diagram, or sketch what they hear.

2 Ask students to use their sketches to explain or tell the main idea of what they heard.

Listen for Patterns of Organization

Have students listen to a paragraph or section you read aloud from the text. Have them tell what kind of organizer they should use for taking notes.

Examples

• Read a paragraph that compares and contrasts; lead students to request a Venn diagram.

• Read a paragraph that presents ideas and explains or supports them; lead students to request a support chart or a web.

Create Oral Practice with Vocabulary

Have students use social studies words to tell about the pictures in their chapters or sections.

Variation Have students use social studies words to ask questions about the pictures in their chapters or sections.

Use Sentence Frames for Oral Elaboration

Help students go beyond one-word or other minimal responses by providing and modeling the use of sentence frames such as these:

For example, _____ .

As a result, _____ .

On the other hand, _____ .

One kind/sort is _____ .

Another group/type/event/example is _____ .

In other words, _____ .

To begin with _____ .

This is why _____ .

Use Sentence Frames for Citing Authorities

Help students back up what they say in oral discussion as well as in persuasive speaking and writing by introducing and modeling sentence frames such as the following:

As the textbook says, _____ .

On page _____ , it says, _____ .

Yesterday, we read that _____ .

You can find this information _____ .

Discuss Actions and Motives of Historical Figures

One way to further students' skill in analyzing literature while increasing comprehension and fostering in-depth understanding of historical events is to examine what people do and why they do it. Help students distinguish between motives that have to do with personal ambition and those that have to do with community, sense of belonging to a group or place, or patriotism.

Frame Oral Questions

Remind students to use the 5W and H questions to think of ways to frame questions about people and events in history or about issues in community and political life. Model using the 5Ws and H to frame oral questions in response to a section or chapter.

Variation Have students use *Solutions Master 19: 5W and H Chart* to jot down ideas for questions before they articulate them.

Solutions Master 19:
5W and H Chart

Create Dramatic Interpretations

Have students plan, write, and stage dramatic interpretations of actual historical events presented in the text and of possible conversations between historical figures. Dramatic, rather than informational, presentations lend themselves well to teaching speaking skills such as the use of tone; varying pitch, pace, and volume; and using meaningful gestures, facial expressions, and body language.

Listen to and Discuss Oral Media

Provide opportunities for students to listen to oral media, such as television or radio news broadcasts, especially when there is a link to the chapter or topic under study. Talk about the ways in which the report helps students create their opinions and whether or not this is a good thing.

Use a Speaking Checklist

Distribute copies of *Solutions Master 34: Speaking Checklist* to help students plan for and reflect on formal speaking occasions.

Use a Listening Checklist

Distribute copies of *Solutions Master 35: Listening Checklist* to help students plan for and reflect on formal listening occasions.

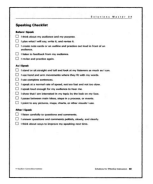

Solutions Master 34:
Speaking Checklist

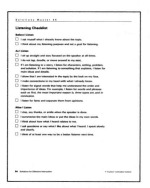

Solutions Master 35:
Listening Checklist

Part Three

Solutions Masters

Cause-and-Effect Diagram

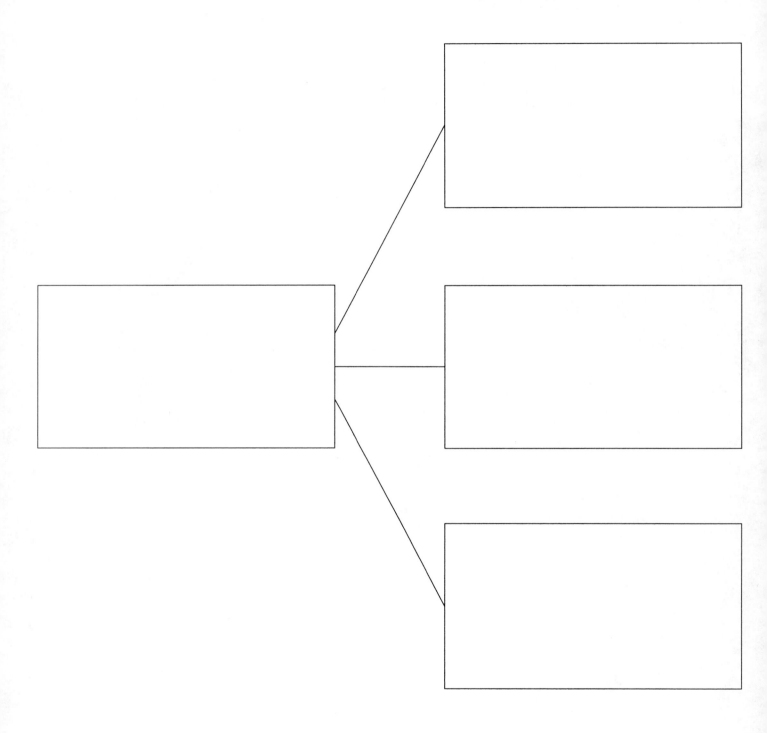

Cause-and-Effect Chain

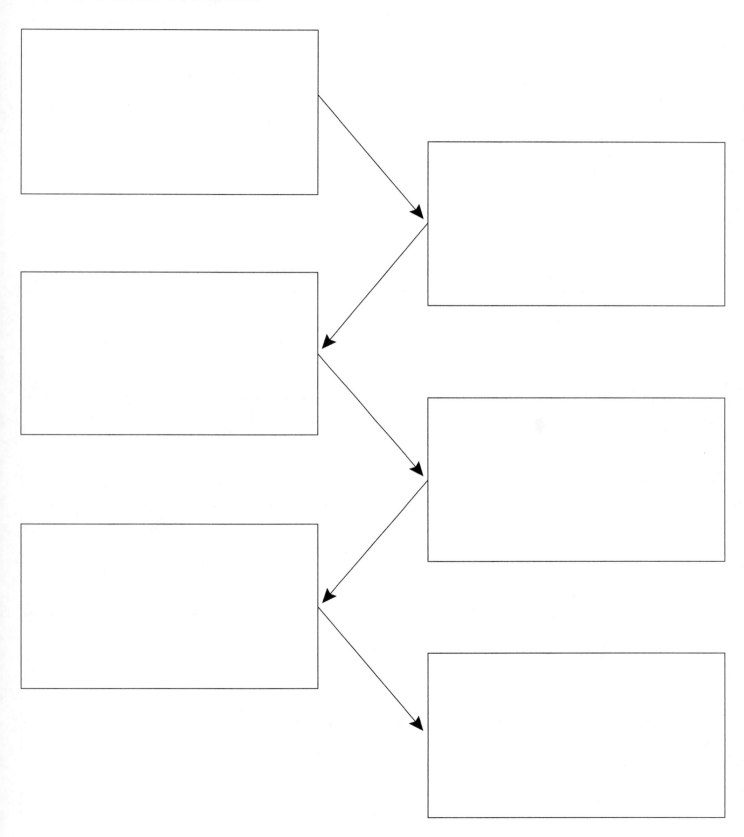

Two-Column Chart

Venn Diagram

Title:_____

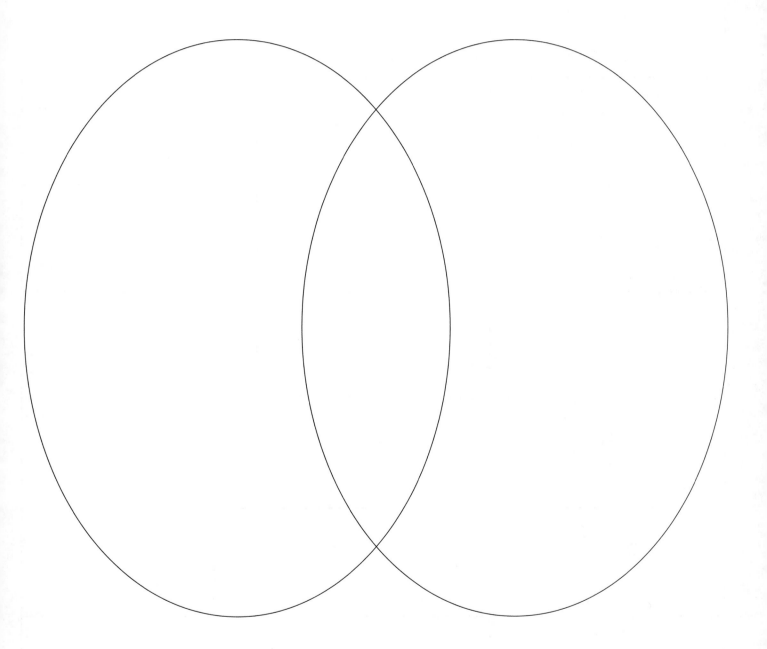

Three-Column Chart

Sequence Chain

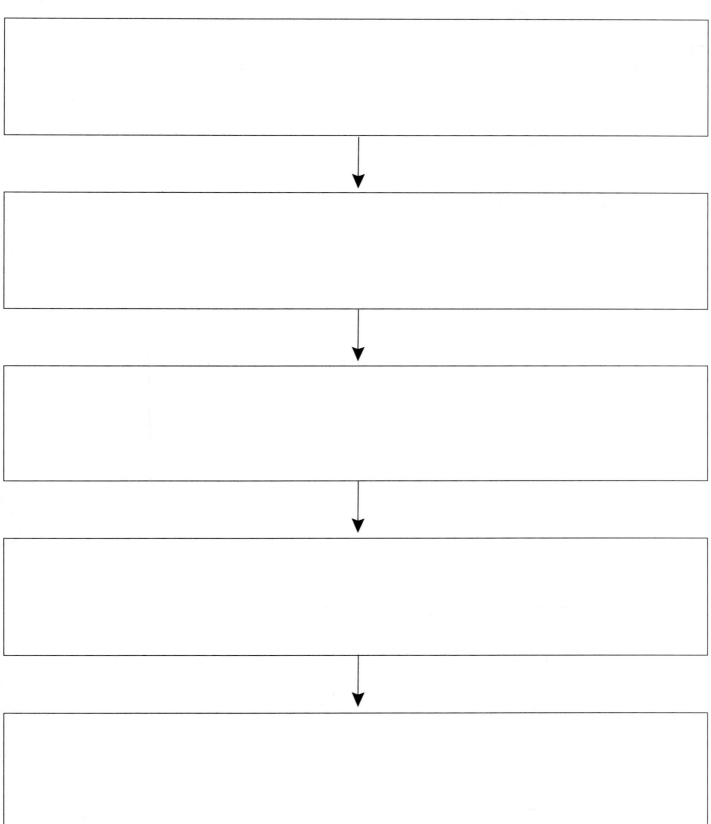

Timeline/Judgment Graphic

Title: _____

Inference/Conclusion Diagram

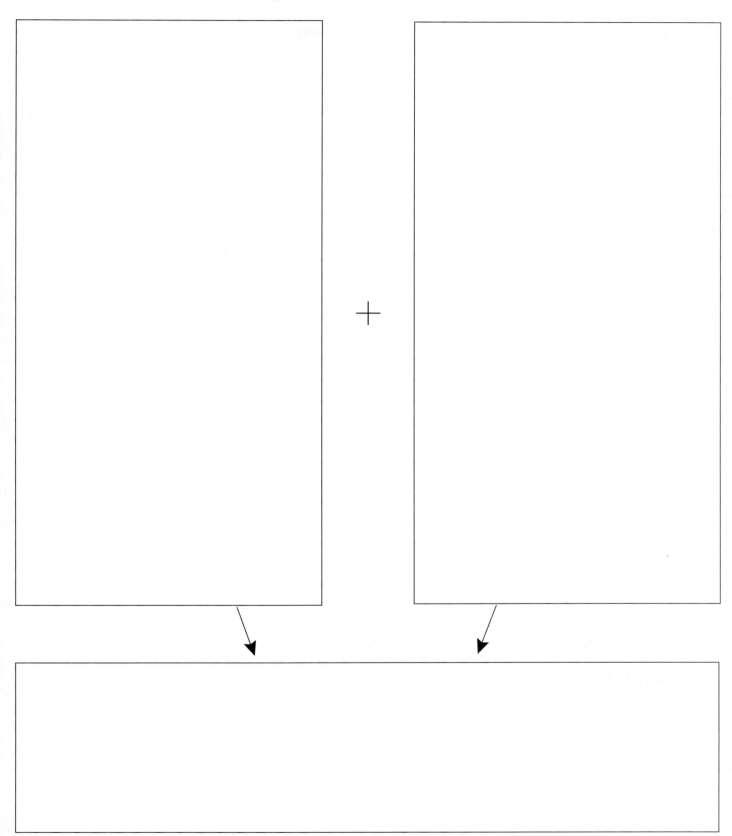

Generalization Diagram

Facts

Facts

Facts

Generalization

Web

Decision Tree/Evaluation Chart

Goal: _____

Choices: _____ **or** _____

Pros	Cons

Pros	Cons

Decision/Evaluation:

Flowchart

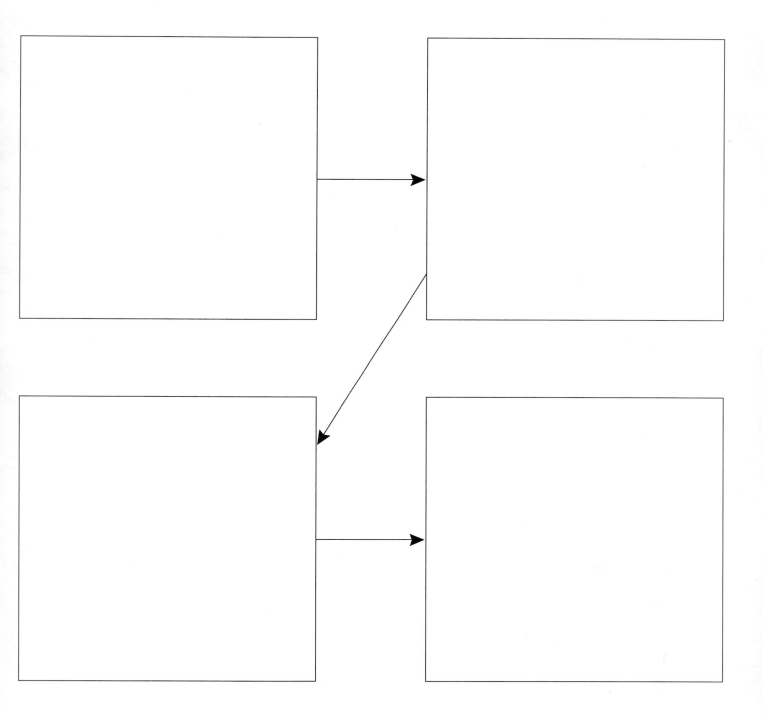

Support Chart

Main Idea or Opinion

Support

Support

Support

Recognize Bias Checklist

Author Does the author belong to a group, hold beliefs, or have interests that would result in a one-sided view of this subject?	
Words Does the author use very negative or very positive words?	
Ideas Does the author exaggerate or understate any facts?	
Completeness Does the author leave out everything that might argue against his or her ideas?	
Tone Does the writing seem full of emotion and based mainly on feelings?	

Beginning-Middle-End Chart

Beginning

Middle

End

Chapter Features Chart

Feature	Example(s)	Purpose
Title		
Introduction		
Section Heads		
Vocabulalry		
Visuals		
Captions		
Summary		
Reading Further		

KWL Chart

I already know . . .	I want to learn . . .	I learned . . .

Make Connections Chart

In my book . . .	In my life . . .

5W and H Chart

Title:_____

Who

What

When

Where

Why

How

Word Knowledge Chart

Word	Know it well	Know it a little	Don't know it

Word Parts Log

Social Studies Word	Prefix	Meaning of Word

Social Studies Word	Root	Meaning of Word

Social Studies Word	Suffix	Meaning of Word

Word Tiers

Word

Definition

Examples

Word

Definition

Examples

Word

Definition

Examples

Word Web

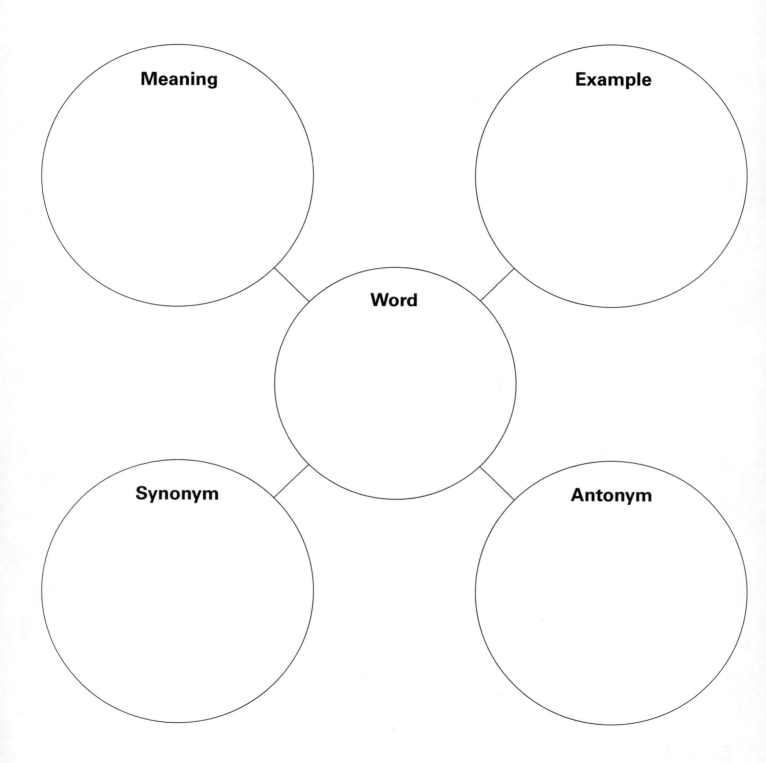

Word Map

Word: _____

Context Sentence	Picture
My Sentence	**Definition**

Word Wheel

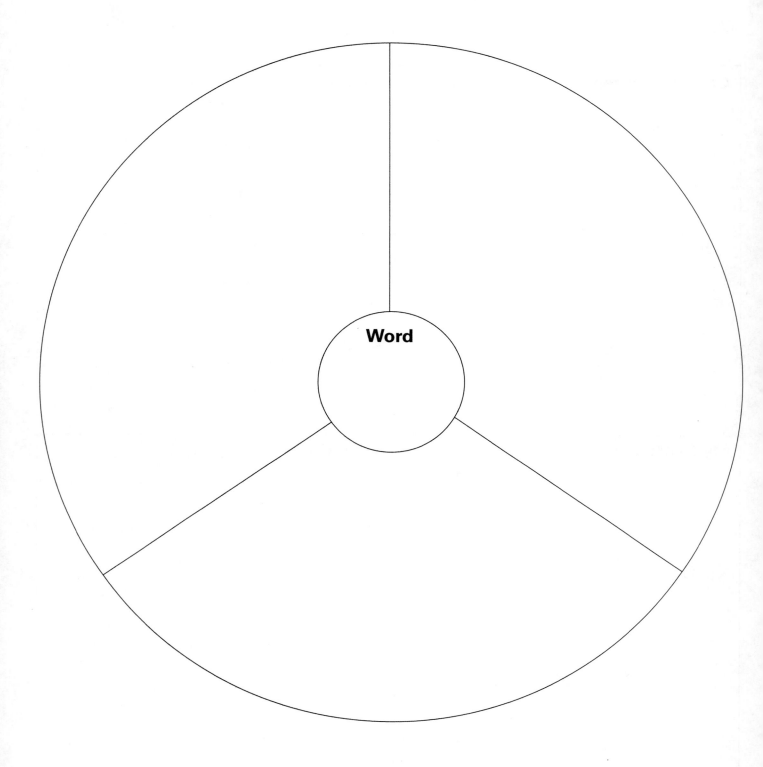

Word Connections Map

Word: _____

Related words	Where I learned the word
How I could use the word	**How I can remember the word**

Writing Process Checklist for Explaining or Describing

Prewriting

☐ I choose one subject or main idea to write about.

☐ I name my audience and think about what they already know or would like to learn.

☐ I name my purpose, such as to explain causes and effects. Then I choose and fill in the kind of graphic organizer that helps me get ideas for that kind of writing.

☐ I use reference materials such as a dictionary, thesaurus, library catalog, encyclopedia, or the Web to get ideas.

☐ I put my ideas in an order that makes sense.

Drafting

☐ I begin in an interesting way and state my topic.

☐ I use my textbook and reference sources to check my information.

☐ I use transition words to connect words, sentences, and paragraphs.

☐ I create paragraphs for compositions. I start with a paragraph for the introduction, one or more paragraphs for the body, and a paragraph for the conclusion.

☐ I start new, indented paragraphs for each new main idea in a composition. My paragraphs contain a topic sentence and explain the main idea.

☐ I use cursive writing or joined letters that everyone can read.

Revising

☐ I reread my work to be sure the meaning and ideas are clear.

☐ I make changes by adding, taking out, or changing the order of ideas.

☐ I meet with my teacher or a classmate to talk about my writing.

☐ I make more changes by adding, taking out, or changing the order of ideas.

☐ I make sure I have the right length and the right spacing, including indented paragraphs and margins.

☐ I read a classmate's writing and give helpful ideas for making it better.

☐ I use the editing and proofreading checklist.

Publishing

☐ I make a final, clean copy of my writing and share it.

Writing Process Checklist for Stories, Steps, or Events

Prewriting

☐ I write down a list of ideas.

☐ I name my audience and think about what they already know or would like to learn.

☐ I choose one main idea to write about.

☐ I name my purpose and use a story map, flowchart, or beginning-middle-end organizer to come up with more ideas about my topic.

Drafting

☐ I begin stories in an interesting way and tell the time and place. I begin steps or events with the first step or event.

☐ I use my textbook and reference sources to check my information about events or steps.

☐ I start new paragraphs when the time, place, or speaker changes or for each new event or step in a process.

☐ I use words such as *first, second, next, then, later,* and *last* to connect words, sentences, and paragraphs.

☐ I use cursive writing or joined letters that everyone can read.

Revising

☐ I reread my work to be sure I tell what happens in order.

☐ I make changes by adding, taking out, or changing the order of ideas.

☐ I meet with my teacher or a classmate to talk about my writing.

☐ I make more changes by adding, taking out, or changing the order of ideas.

☐ I make sure I have the right length and the right spacing, including indented paragraphs and margins.

☐ I read a classmate's writing and give helpful ideas for making it better.

☐ I use the editing and proofreading checklist.

Publishing

☐ I make a final, clean copy of my writing and share my work.

Story Map

Characters
Setting
Conflict/Problem
Events of the Plot
1.
2.
3.
Ending/Solution

Composition Plan for Explaining or Describing

Introduction

My topic and central idea about it:

Body Paragraph

Topic sentence about my central idea:

Supporting ideas and details:

Body Paragraph

Topic sentence about my central idea:

Supporting ideas and details:

Body Paragraph

Topic sentence about my central idea:

Supporting ideas and details:

Conclusion

Summary and final thought:

Composition Plan for Persuading

Introduction

My opinion:

Body Paragraph

Reason 1 for my opinion:

Explanation and evidence:

Body Paragraph

Reason 2 for my opinion:

Explanation and evidence:

Body Paragraph

Reason 3 for my opinion:

Explanation and evidence:

Conclusion

Summary and call to action:

Peer Revising Checklist

When I am the writer,

☐ I write and revise before I give my reader my draft.

☐ I give my reader a clean copy of my draft.

☐ I tell my reader what problems I am still working on.

☐ I give my reader plenty of time to read and respond.

☐ I listen carefully to my reader's ideas.

☐ I think about what my reader says before I answer.

☐ I ask questions about any comments I do not understand.

When I am the reader,

☐ I read carefully. I take as much time as I need. If I need to, I reread.

☐ I ask questions about things that I don't understand.

☐ I begin by telling the writer what works well. I tell exactly what is good, such as a clear main idea, a clear topic sentence, or a specific word choice.

☐ I tell exactly what to change, such as a sentence that is off the topic or does not make sense.

☐ I am polite and honest.

Editing and Proofreading Checklist

Paragraphs

☐ I use a topic sentence in paragraphs that explain. I follow the topic sentence with examples, facts, explanation, and other details that support the topic sentence.

☐ I indent my paragraphs.

Sentences and Grammar

☐ I write complete sentences with subjects and verbs that agree.

☐ I check all the verbs in my sentences to be sure they are in the right tense (past, present, or future). I make sure to use regular and irregular verbs correctly.

☐ I combine short, related sentences into longer sentences using words such as *and* and *but*.

Capital Letters and Punctuation

☐ I use capital letters for place names, holidays, historical periods, special events, organizations, newspapers, and magazines.

☐ I use italics (when I word process) or underlining (when I write by hand) for the titles of books.

☐ I use commas in dates, locations, and addresses, and with groups of three or more items.

☐ I use apostrophes in contractions and with naming words to show ownership.

☐ I use commas and quotation marks where they are needed in dialogue and titles.

Spelling

☐ I check all the words that sound the same for correct spelling, such as *their, they're,* and *there.*

☐ I use what I have learned about syllables and about roots, prefixes, and suffixes to spell words correctly.

☐ I check my spelling with a spell-checker and the dictionary.

Speaking Checklist

Before I Speak

☐ I think about my audience and my purpose.

☐ I plan what I will say, write it, and revise it.

☐ I create note cards or an outline and practice out loud in front of an audience.

☐ I listen to feedback from my audience.

☐ I revise and practice again.

As I Speak

☐ I stand or sit straight and tall and look at my listeners as much as I can.

☐ I use hand and arm movements where they fit with my words.

☐ I use complete sentences.

☐ I speak at a normal rate of speed, not too fast and not too slow.

☐ I speak loud enough for my audience to hear me.

☐ I show that I am interested in my topic by the look on my face.

☐ I pause between main ideas, steps in a process, or events.

☐ I point to any pictures, maps, charts, or other visuals I use.

After I Speak

☐ I listen carefully to questions and comments.

☐ I answer questions and comments politely, slowly, and clearly.

☐ I think about ways to improve my speaking next time.

Listening Checklist

Before I Listen

☐ I ask myself what I already know about the topic.

☐ I think about my listening purpose and set a goal for listening.

As I Listen

☐ I sit up straight and stay focused on the speaker at all times.

☐ I do not tap, doodle, or move around in my seat.

☐ If I am listening to a story, I listen for characters, setting, problem, and solution. If I am listening to something that explains, I listen for main ideas and details.

☐ I show that I am interested in the topic by the look on my face.

☐ I make connections in my head with what I already know.

☐ I listen for signal words that help me understand the order and importance of ideas. For example, I listen for words and phrases such as *first, the most important reason is, three types are,* and *in conclusion.*

☐ I listen for facts and separate them from opinions.

After I Listen

☐ I clap, say thanks, or smile when the speaker is done.

☐ I summarize the main ideas or put the ideas in my own words.

☐ I think about how what I heard relates to me.

☐ I ask questions or say what I like about what I heard. I speak slowly and clearly.

☐ I think of at least one way to be a better listener next time.

Part Four

Differentiating Instruction

Best Practices for English Language Learners

English language learners are those students in our classrooms whose native language is not English. No matter how capable, creative, and motivated these students are, their developing language skills can interfere with their academic success. The following best practices help address issues related to English language learners and support student success in the general education classroom.

Set up your classroom for success

- Establish a classroom environment in which students feel safe to answer questions, share ideas, and volunteer for classroom activities.
- Develop and state consistent classroom routines.
- Display pictures and charts to support content.
- Create a word wall that includes key vocabulary, definitions, and pictures.
- Identify language goals as well as content goals for your lessons.
- Incorporate materials that reflect diversity.

Build additional background knowledge (schema) to help students connect to content

- Use a visual, illustrated story, or short dramatic role-play to build background knowledge, preview the lesson, and elicit personal responses.
- Help students make connections with their personal experiences.

Pre-teach vocabulary

- Present vocabulary practice activities that incorporate multiple learning styles.
- Encourage the use of flashcards.
- Include words, definitions, and pictures on your classroom word wall.
- Allow students to use dual language dictionaries as needed to understand new vocabulary.

Teach understanding of concepts and big ideas

- Model and encourage the use of a method such as concept mapping for organizing content around big ideas.
- Provide frequent repetition.
- Use concept mastery strategies based on providing examples and non-examples and have students build the definition of a concept.

- Support the teaching of content with sketches, diagrams, and other visuals.
- Integrate social studies content into language arts instruction and vice versa.

Develop fluency

- When students give a one-word answer, model elaboration, or ask for elaboration, depending on the student's level of proficiency.
- Have students paraphrase what other students say.
- Provide multiple opportunities for pair-share and small group discussion before sharing in a large group.
- Structure classroom procedures so that all students regularly have the opportunity for oral participation.

Provide support for the text

- Teach students how to read the text using built-in text supports (glossary, chapter summaries, etc.).
- Model how chapter features (chapter title, section headings, the summary, etc.) provide you with a content overview and assist you with locating information.
- Model and emphasize looking at text in small, manageable sections.
- Highlight and annotate key vocabulary for other reading materials, such as primary sources, trade books, or other supplemental texts.

Organize information to support understanding of content

- Model how to use graphic organizers to record information.
- Present new information in a format that organizes and summarizes ideas, such as a chart or diagram.
- Have students draw or find visuals that will make content more understandable to them.

Assess frequently

- Check for understanding throughout the lesson.
- Create assessments that ask students to demonstrate their learning in ways that call on a variety of abilities (for example, drawing a picture, writing a poem, creating a rap).
- Show models of finished products prior to product completion.
- Use an exit ticket or question-of-the-day strategy to make sure students are getting important content.
- Brainstorm as a class or group for ideas that can be incorporated into products.
- Provide students with choices about how they would like to demonstrate learning.
- Assess progress on individual lessons instead of relying only on a test at the end of a chapter.

Find ways to create a strong school-home connection

- Provide opportunities for students to share work with parents and elicit parental feedback.
- Invite parents to class to see how instruction supports student learning and how parents can reinforce learning at home.
- Send home important information in the languages of your students.
- Provide meeting times with parents that can fit their schedules.

Best Practices for Students with Special Needs

Learners with special needs are those students in our classrooms who have learning and/or behavioral disabilities that interfere with their academic success or who struggle with basic learning tasks required at this grade level. Some of these students have Individualized Education Plans (IEPs) that specify the modifications required in the general education classroom. The following best practices include modifications to help foster academic success.

Set up your classroom for success

- Display pictures and charts to support content.
- Use flexible grouping to make sure that special education students have the opportunity to work with learners of different abilities.

Purposely set expectations for, and connect with, your students

- Find ways that are unrelated to academic ability to highlight what these students do well.
- Establish clear and consistent rules and classroom procedures so students know what to expect each day.
- Help students create a system for staying organized throughout the day (notebooks, homework folder, daily assignment planner, etc.).
- Provide opportunities for special needs learners to be recognized in front of their peers for achievement.

Check your lesson plan for preview, activity, and process

- Include a preview for each lesson that will connect to the student, as well as set a purpose for learning.
- Check for understanding throughout, as well as at the end of, a lesson by using a think-pair-share strategy or having students repeat in their own words important ideas from the lesson.

Use multiple modalities (oral, visual, kinesthetic) to deliver content

- Give information about assignments and class content both orally and in writing.
- Support content with experiential activities and visuals to foster understanding.
- Reinforce content through multiple activities using different learning styles.

Organize each lesson around a powerful graphic organizer

- Use diagrams and charts.
- Create graphic organizers with visuals that provide a structure for students to connect with content.

Modify student handouts and reading assignments

- Photocopy text pages and highlight key content.
- Identify page numbers on assignments that help students locate information more efficiently in the text.
- Create cloze assignments that allow students to fill in missing words instead of writing lengthy answers.
- Reduce the number of items that need to be completed.

Allow alternative methods of demonstrating understanding

- Offer choice in products that involve different intelligences (writing assignments, artistic assignments, technology assignments).
- Group students to allow special education students to complete products with other learners.
- Provide alternative assignments for assessment, such as writing a postcard instead of a letter or drawing a poster instead of writing a composition.
- Provide extended time for product completion as needed or dictated by the student's IEP.

Adapt chapter tests

- Provide a word bank.
- Underline key clue words in question stems.
- Eliminate one of the choices on a multiple-choice test.
- Refer to a student's IEP for test modifications such as reading aloud.

Find ways to create a strong school-home connection

- Contact parents frequently.
- Share positive comments prior to concerns when talking with parents.
- Provide parents with suggested strategies to support student learning.

Best Practices for Enrichment

Enrichment is appropriate for those students in our classrooms who master content at a more rapid pace than their peers do, as well as for students who find the content of particular chapters especially engaging. Enrichment opportunities should provide different work, not just more work: no matter how highly capable, creative, and motivated these students may be, they still rely on their teacher to facilitate meaningful learning. The following best practices help support students who are ready for enrichment opportunities.

Pre-assess knowledge
- Check what students know before a lesson and then teach beyond that knowledge.

Compact the curriculum
- Have students spend their time on meaningful activities rather than working with content they already know.
- Make sure the content is covered but allow for enrichment, such as having an anchor activity for all and then having students extend learning by studying the topic from another perspective, at the next step in the process, or at a higher level of thinking.

Vary text and resources
- Provide students with supplementary texts at multiple levels, including trade books and primary sources.
- Share TCI Enrichment Readings and other Online Resources for delving into content in greater depth.

Spiral discussions that lead to higher level questioning
- Purposefully develop questions at all levels on Bloom's taxonomy during the course of a lesson (that is, ask recall and comprehension questions as well as questions requiring application, analysis, synthesis, and evaluation).

Group students flexibly
- Within a heterogeneously grouped classroom, allow students who are ready for enrichment to work together.
- Structure groups in various ways, such as by interest, topic, ability, or student-selected groupings.
- Keep groups fluid, based on specific instructional needs.

Incorporate multiple learning styles into your classroom
- Ensure that students can use their strengths, talents, and interests in various areas to access information and demonstrate their learning.

Use tiered assignments
- Create assignments at multiple levels to meet the needs of diverse learners. These assignments should meet lesson goals but also ensure that all learners are engaged in meaningful, challenging work.

- Present varied levels of instruction based on the content presented, the process by which students learn content, and the products students create to demonstrate learning.

Provide independent project opportunities

- Allow students who are ready for enrichment opportunities to complete independent study work of greater breadth and depth than what is being presented to other students.
- Set up learning centers offering project choices, starter ideas, and resources.

Apply content to other areas

- Help students make connections to other topics and disciplines (for example, when learning about the Civil War, have students read a historical novel about the war, or have students compile, display, and analyze data from the Civil War, such as data about railway tracks or factory output).

Maximize opportunities for students to understand what they have to learn rather than what they already know

- Make students aware that undertaking enrichment activities is a positive opportunity to learn more.
- Students ready for enrichment should not always be assigned to serve as tutors to students needing support.
- While students ready for enrichment may be able to work more independently, they still need their teacher to provide insights and guidance, as well as instruction in various tasks and activities, such as organization, study skills, locating resources, and taking notes.